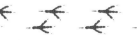

BALD EAGLE

NATIONAL GEOGRAPHIC KiDS

BIRD GUIDE
OF NORTH AMERICA

THE BEST BIRDING BOOK FOR KIDS FROM A NATIONAL GEOGRAPHIC BIRD EXPERT

JONATHAN ALDERFER

NATIONAL GEOGRAPHIC
WASHINGTON, D.C.

Contents

p. 38
Anna's
Hummingbird

p. 96
Osprey

p. 128
Great Blue
Heron

BIRDS ARE BEAUTIFUL
AND AWE-INSPIRING WILD ANIMALS THAT LIVE EVERYWHERE WE DO.

Many people get so interested in birds that they become bird-watchers (also called birders). They like to learn about birds so that they can identify the birds they see, or just to be entertained. Did you know that bird-watching is one of the most popular hobbies in North America? About 44 million people watch birds, just in the United States. There's a good chance that someone in your family could be a bird-watcher.

But bird-watching isn't just for grown-ups. Lots of kids are bird-watchers, too. A great way to get started is to put up a feeder so you can watch birds in your backyard—check out the simple plan to make your own bird feeder in the back of this book. It's easy to get hooked on birds, and soon you'll want to look for birds beyond your backyard.

Bird-watching, it's like going on a treasure hunt—keep your eyes and ears open and you might just find something really cool. Keep a list of what you see, and add to your collection of bird sightings throughout the year.

Join me on a tour of the more than 150 bird species in this book. You'll find all kinds of birds inside, from huge predators, like the Bald Eagle, to tiny hummingbirds, and everything in between. All the birds are divided into 10 different habitats—like deserts, prairies, and even back-yards. Look for a habitat that matches where you live. That's a good place to start. And welcome to the club!

—Jonathan Alderfer

ROSEATE SPOONBILL

How to Use This Book!

FIFTY BIRDS ARE PROFILED THROUGHOUT THIS BOOK, WITH AN ADDITIONAL 102 BIRDS INTRODUCED IN MINI-PROFILES AT THE END OF EACH SECTION.

THE TITLE CLEARLY SHOWS YOU WHICH HABITAT YOU WILL READ ABOUT.

EACH SECTION IS COLOR-CODED WITH A TAB TO HELP YOU KEEP TRACK OF WHAT SECTION YOU ARE IN.

Western Backyard Birds

TO FIND OUT THE NAME OF THE BIRD SHOWN ON EACH OPENER, LOOK FOR EACH BIRD'S COMMON NAME.

ANNA'S HUMMINGBIRD

THE PHOTOS ON THE HABITAT SPREADS ILLUSTRATE AN EXAMPLE OF WHAT EACH HABITAT LOOKS LIKE.

THE BIRDS YOU WILL READ ABOUT IN EACH SECTION ARE INTRODUCED ON THESE SPREADS. PHOTOS OF THE BIRDS ARE PLACED IN LOCATIONS WHERE YOU ARE LIKELY TO SEE THEM WHEN BIRD-WATCHING.

Southern Swamp and Bayou
HABITAT

BARRED OWL

SNOWY EGRET

WOOD DUCK

LIMPKIN

A UNIQUE PLACE TO LIVE

A swamp is a low-lying wooded area that is usually flooded with overflow from a nearby river or lake, and is full of plant and animal life. Tupelo, cypress, and other types of trees and vegetation get lots of water and grow thick. Bayous, found along the Gulf Coast, can be a slow-moving river or stream, or a marshy lake or wetland. Many types of animals—crawfish, shrimp, catfish, alligators, frogs, and a great variety of insects—are abundant in swamps and bayous, and so are the birds that feed on them.

110

111

INTRODUCTORY TEXT PROVIDES BASIC INFORMATION ABOUT EACH HABITAT.

YOU WILL FIND EACH BIRD'S COMMON NAME IN THE UPPER LEFT CORNER OF EACH PROFILE SPREAD.

FIND OUT THE DIFFERENT TYPES OF SOUNDS BIRDS MAKE IN THIS SECTION.

BIRDS HAVE A VARIED DIET. FIND OUT WHAT TYPES OF FOOD EACH SPECIES EATS IN THIS SECTION.

THE YELLOW BOXES INCLUDE FUN FACTS ABOUT EACH SPECIES.

THIS SECTION POINTS OUT DIFFERENT BODY PARTS AND, IN MANY CASES, THE PURPOSE OF EACH.

THE MAP SHOWS EACH BIRD'S RANGE WITH DIFFERENT COLORS. THE KEY EXPLAINS WHAT EACH COLOR ON THE MAP ILLUSTRATES.

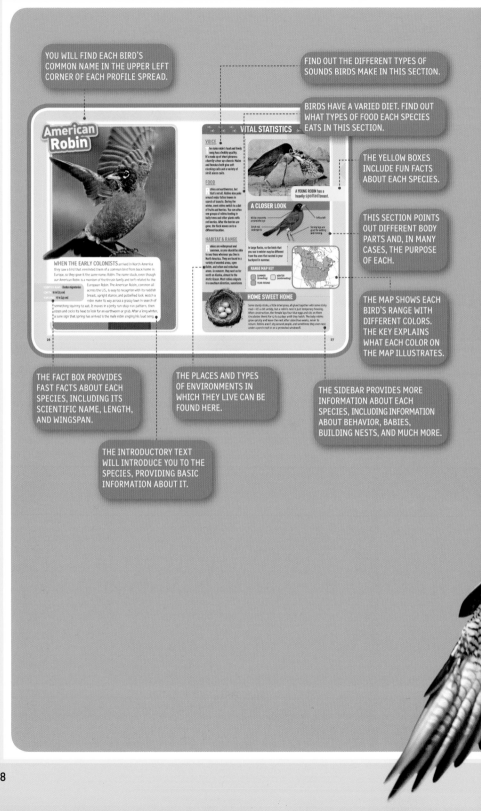

THE FACT BOX PROVIDES FAST FACTS ABOUT EACH SPECIES, INCLUDING ITS SCIENTIFIC NAME, LENGTH, AND WINGSPAN.

THE PLACES AND TYPES OF ENVIRONMENTS IN WHICH THEY LIVE CAN BE FOUND HERE.

THE SIDEBAR PROVIDES MORE INFORMATION ABOUT EACH SPECIES, INCLUDING INFORMATION ABOUT BEHAVIOR, BABIES, BUILDING NESTS, AND MUCH MORE.

THE INTRODUCTORY TEXT WILL INTRODUCE YOU TO THE SPECIES, PROVIDING BASIC INFORMATION ABOUT IT.

THE TITLE OF EACH OF THESE SPREADS IS LOCATED IN THE UPPER LEFT CORNER.

TEXT BLOCKS NEXT TO THE TITLE INTRODUCE THE GROUP OF BIRDS YOU WILL READ ABOUT.

THE TEXT BLOCKS THAT ACCOMPANY EACH BIRD PHOTO PROVIDE A BRIEF EXPLANATION OF EACH SPECIES.

FOR FAST FACTS ABOUT EACH SPECIES FOUND ON THESE SPREADS, CHECK OUT THE FACT BOXES. HERE YOU WILL FIND THE SCIENTIFIC NAME, LENGTH, AND WINGSPAN FOR EACH BIRD.

Mini-Profiles

EASTERN BACKYARD

Here are 12 more species of birds that live in eastern backyards. Many of these birds love to eat seeds from a bird feeder or scattered on the ground.

MOURNING DOVE
Zenaida macroura

There are the same number of Mourning Doves living in the U.S. as there are people—about 350 million. They live in open areas including suburban yards. Listen for the dove's slow, mournful call, oowoo-woo-woo-woo, and the whistling sound made by its wings when it bursts into flight. You can attract doves to your backyard by scattering birdseed on the ground.

The colorful Red-shouldered Hawk is a very vocal bird with a loud screaming call, KEE-ohh. When you hear its call, look up to see it soaring over wooded backyards. To catch its prey, the hawk perches quietly at the edge of the woods and then pounces down on small mammals and reptiles.

DOWNY WOODPECKER
Picoides pubescens

The tiny Downy Woodpecker—the smallest woodpecker in North America—is common across the continent from Maine to California. The Downy is the woodpecker most likely to show up at a bird feeder, where it prefers to eat suet (animal fat, usually mixed with seeds or fruit). Like most woodpeckers, it is black and white, although the male has a spot of bright red on the back of his head. This bird is small enough to search for food on thin branches and weed stems that couldn't support its larger, similar-looking cousin, the Hairy Woodpecker. The Downy's call is a sharp, high-pitched pik!

RED-SHOULDERED HAWK
Buteo lineatus

EASTERN PHOEBE
Sayornis phoebe

From spring through fall this medium-size flycatcher is often seen around houses, barns, and sheds. You might hear it call out its name, fee-bee, before you see it. Phoebes like to nest in sheltered locations and often choose an open porch if it has a ledge that will support its nest. The Eastern Phoebe returns to its northern breeding locations early in the spring. Its body is dark brown above and whitish below. Even when perched, it doesn't stay still—it constantly pumps its tail up and down.

If you see a small gray-and-white bird climbing nimbly up, down, and around a tree trunk, chances are good that you've spotted a White-breasted Nuthatch. The nuthatch has an extra-long hind claw that helps it get a grip in any position. It lives year-round in woods and wooded backyards and is crazy about suet feeders. Its call is a low-pitched nasal yank.

CAROLINA WREN
Thryothorus ludovicianus

The Carolina Wren is small and chunky, with a long tail and long bill curved downward. Its plumage is a buffy orange below and reddish brown above with a bold white eye stripe. The Carolina Wren has lots of personality. If you leave a back porch door open for a few hours, a Carolina Wren will probably poke inside for a look. When not poking around where people live, it searches in shrubs, brush piles, and berry patches for insects and spiders. The male is a masterful singer and may sing dozens of different song variations.

WHITE-BREASTED NUTHATCH
Sitta carolinensis

30

PEREGRINE FALCON

RUSSIA

ARCTIC OCEAN

165°
150°
135°
120°
105°
90°
75°
60°
45°
30°
15°

Greenland

DENMARK

ALASKA
(UNITED STATES)

YUKON

NORTHWEST TERRITORIES

NUNAVUT

ARCTIC CIRCLE

60°

BRITISH COLUMBIA

ALBERTA

SASK.

MANITOBA

C A N A D A

QUEBEC

NEWFOUNDLAND AND LABRADOR

ONTARIO

WASH.

MONTANA

NORTH DAKOTA

MINN.

MICHIGAN

ME.
N.B. P.E.I.
NOVA SCOTIA

45°

OREGON

IDAHO

WYOMING

SOUTH DAKOTA

WIS.

VT.
N.Y.

NEW HAMPSHIRE
MASSACHUSETTS
RHODE ISLAND
CONNECTICUT
DELAWARE

CALIFORNIA

NEVADA

UTAH

COLORADO

NEBRASKA

IOWA

ILL.
IND.

OHIO

PA.

N.J.

MD.

ARIZONA

U N I T E D   S T A T E S

KANSAS

MO.

KY.

W. VA.
VA.

NEW MEXICO

OKLA.

ARK.

TENN.

N.C.

S.C.

TEXAS

MISS.
ALA.
GA.

ATLANTIC OCEAN

30°

LA.

FLORIDA

M E X I C O

BAHAMAS

TROPIC OF CANCER

C U B A

W e s t   I n d i e s

PACIFIC OCEAN

HAITI

DOMINICAN REPUBLIC

15°

JAMAICA

BELIZE

GUATEMALA

HONDURAS

EL SALVADOR

NICARAGUA

Azimuthal Equidistant Projection

0   400   800 MILES

0   400   800 KILOMETERS

COSTA RICA

PANAMA

SOUTH AMERICA

EQUATOR

105°

90°

75°

0°

ABBREVIATIONS

Ala.	Alabama	N.J.	New Jersey
Ark.	Arkansas	N.Y.	New York
Ga.	Georgia	Okla.	Oklahoma
Ill.	Illinois	Pa.	Pennsylvania
Ind.	Indiana	P.E.I.	Prince Edward Island
Ky.	Kentucky	Sask.	Saskatchewan
La.	Louisiana	S.C.	South Carolina
Md.	Maryland	Tenn.	Tennessee
Me.	Maine	Va.	Virginia
Minn.	Minnesota	Vt.	Vermont
Miss.	Mississippi	Wash.	Washington
Mo.	Missouri	Wis.	Wisconsin
N.B.	New Brunswick	W. Va.	West Virginia
N.C.	North Carolina		

RANGE MAPS

The following is a sample of the range maps and map keys you will find on the bird profile pages throughout this book.

RANGE MAP KEY

SUMMER (breeding)

WINTER (nonbreeding)

MIGRATION

YEAR-ROUND

SAMPLE RANGE MAP

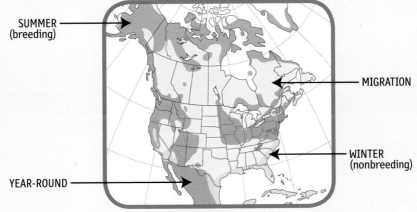

SUMMER (breeding)

MIGRATION

WINTER (nonbreeding)

YEAR-ROUND

Range Map of the Peregrine Falcon

Getting Started as a Birder

Common Grackle

Most kids are interested in nature and love to explore. You are one of those nature-loving kids if you are reading this book—that's a no-brainer. If you are wondering how to start exploring the world of birds living around you, this book will help.

WHERE ARE THE BIRDS?

HABITAT

Birds have favorite places, just like people. Although some birds seem to live just about everywhere, most birds prefer a specific type of place—or habitat. That's because the habitat—the land and plants of an area—provides them with what they need to live a healthy life. All of the birds described in this book are divided into 10 different habitats because habitat is a great clue to what types of bird you might see in a particular area. For instance, sandpipers are found on mudflats and beaches, not up in trees with wood-peckers, of course!

Many species—especially smaller birds—don't move around too much. The same chickadees that come to your feeder in fall and winter probably nest nearby in the summer. But birds have wings and can fly long distances. Some birds, like hawks and vultures, might fly many miles every day searching for food. Other birds migrate long distances, but once they get to where they want to nest or to spend the winter, most of them stay put for months.

"BIRDY" PLACES

Even within a specific habitat, there are places that are especially attractive to birds: places that have lots of food or that are safe to nest or to roost overnight. If you want to see lots of birds, be on the lookout for these special locations:

• **Edges.** Anywhere the habitat changes from one type to another, such as the place where a forest stops and a field begins.

• **Sheltered Areas.** Birds are attracted to small areas out of the wind because they tend to be warmer, especially in winter.

• **Water.** Water is a magnet for all kinds of birds in all kinds of places, from deserts to mountains.

• **Your Backyard.** A backyard or common area where you can put up a bird feeder and birdbath is likely to attract a large number of birds. There are plans in the back of this book that show you how to make a bird feeder.

WHAT BIRD IS IT?

BE A BIRD DETECTIVE

Once you are watching a bird, it's time to play detective. Each bird you see is a mystery for you to solve. And like any detective, you have to search for clues and gather evidence to help you solve each mystery. You can watch and identify birds without binoculars, but you'll get a much better look at the bird by using binoculars.

WHAT ARE ITS FIELD MARKS?

"Field mark" is the term that bird-watchers use to describe something unique about a particular species of bird. Field marks are the clues that will help you put a name to a mystery bird. The first thing that most people notice about a bird is its color, but there are a lot of other field marks. Sometimes you need only one clue to identify a mystery bird, but often you need several clues to find the answer. Here's a list of the most important types of field marks to consider:

- **Color**
- **Size**
- **Shape**
- **Behavior**
- **Song**

WHAT COLOR IS THE BIRD?

There are completely red birds (male cardinals) and completely black birds (crows), but most birds are a combination of colors. Remember to look at the pattern of dark and light areas on a bird, as well as its colors. Can you see streaks on the chest, spots on the wings, or a white tail? Noticing these patterns can help you tell similar birds apart.

HOW BIG IS THE BIRD?

It helps to compare a new bird to a common one you already know. For instance, is it bigger than a robin or smaller than a robin? Try thinking of it this way:

- **Tiny**—Hummingbirds
- **Small**—Sparrows, chickadees, wrens
- **Medium**—Robins, jays, blackbirds
- **Large**—Crows, hawks, ducks
- **Huge**—Eagles, herons, pelicans, swans

WHAT SHAPE IS THE BIRD?

Is it tall and slender with long legs for wading in the water? Does it have a crest like a Blue Jay or Northern Cardinal? Or is it small with short legs for hopping on the ground? What is the shape of its bill? You might not be able to give your mystery bird a name just by looking at its shape, but you can often figure out what type of bird it is. For instance, that tall bird with long legs might be a heron and that small bird with short legs hopping on the ground is probably a sparrow.

Western Meadowlark

Bushtit

WHAT IS THE BIRD DOING?

How a bird is behaving or what it is doing can be good clues. If you see a medium-size, black-and-white bird clinging to a tree trunk, it's probably a woodpecker. A large bird soaring high in the sky is probably a hawk or vulture.

USE YOUR EARS

Songs and call notes can be as important as visual clues. Each bird species has its own special songs and calls. Some birds have such memorable songs that they are named for them. Chickadees really do go *chick-a-dee-dee-dee* and the Eastern Phoebe calls out *fee-bee*. Some experienced birders can iden-tify birds just by their songs and calls. Even if you don't recognize a bird's song, it's a great clue to where it may be hiding.

BINOCULARS AND OTHER GEAR

BINOCULARS

It is possible to look at birds without binocu-lars—for example, at a window feeder or a park where the birds have become tame. But, almost always, binoculars help you see birds much more clearly. Through binoculars the birds will appear close up, so you can see details. And with binoculars, you can easily see birds that are flying high in the sky or feeding up in the treetops.

Many families have a pair of binoculars that are used at sporting events or concerts.

While these may not be ideal binoculars for looking at birds, they are better than no binoculars at all. Ask if you can borrow them and how to adjust them to your eyes, and promise to take good care of them.

HOW TO USE BINOCULARS

First, find a bird with your naked eyes. Then, *without taking your eyes off the bird,* lift the binoculars to your eyes. Usually you'll see the bird right away. Tip: It's almost impossible to find a bird by scanning the trees while looking through the binoculars. And remember to always keep the binoculars strap around your neck.

KEEPING TRACK

A small notebook and a pencil are useful, but not essential. Jot down the date and place and what birds you saw, and any details about the bird that interest you. Later, if you start a life list (a list of all the species you have ever seen), you will have a record of the birds you have already seen. For starters, try keeping a list of the birds you see in your backyard taped to the refrigerator and update it with new birds as you see them.

FIELD GUIDE BOOKS

You can bring along this book when you go bird-watching, but it would be better to concentrate on watching the birds when you're outside and look the birds up in the book later on. There are more than 150 birds described in this book, but you will also see birds that aren't in this book. As you get more involved in watching birds, you may want to get a field guide with more species in it, like *The National Geographic Backyard Guide to Birds*, or the granddaddy of all field guides: *The National Geographic Field Guide to Birds of North America*.

CLOTHING

Clothing in bright colors, bold patterns, or white can scare birds. If possible, wear tan, dark green or olive, dark blue, or brown. Avoid noisy nylon jackets or pants that make loud, swishy noises when you walk. Wearing a baseball-style hat will shield your eyes from the sun's glare and make it easier to see birds in the treetops or soaring high in a sunny sky. Don't wear sunglasses, though; they make it impossible to see birds hiding in darker places.

PLAY BY THE RULES

• **Be quiet and careful.** If you make noise, talk in a loud voice, or get too close, the birds will get scared and fly away. Be stealthy and sneak up on birds, so they stay put and you can look at them. You can get fairly close if you try!

• **Don't disturb nesting birds, their nests, eggs, or baby birds.** If you come upon a baby bird on the ground that is not yet able to fly, leave it where it is. Chances are, the baby bird's mother knows where it is and will come to feed it. If it has left the nest, it may be close to being able to fly. Although a baby bird that has left the nest too soon may not make it, baby birds that are "rescued" by people often die. If you're in doubt, call your local Audubon Society or a veterinarian.

• **Respect private and public property.** Ask permission before going onto private property—like yards, country clubs, or private beaches—to look at birds. While in parks or nature preserves, stay on paths, trails, or boardwalks, and don't do anything to damage the environment. When there are no trash cans around, put your litter in your pocket or backpack and take it home with you.

• **HAVE FUN!**

Northern Cardinal

Red-tailed Hawk

AMERICAN ROBIN

Eastern
Backyard
Birds

Eastern Backyard

HABITAT

NORTHERN CARDINAL

BLACK-CAPPED CHICKADEE

ALWAYS SOMETHING NEW!

Birds love the variety of trees and bushes found in eastern backyards, which provide lots of places to nest, gather food, and hide from predators. By adding a bird feeder and a birdbath to your yard, many species will become year-round residents. Some species will make your backyard their home just during the summer, others will pass through twice a year on migration, and a few will be there only in winter. That's what keeps backyard birding fun—something new is always happening!

RUBY-THROATED
HUMMINGBIRD

BLUE JAY

AMERICAN ROBIN

Ruby-throated Hummingbird

RUBY-THROATED Hummingbirds are the only species of hummingbird living on the East Coast. These tiny birds can sometimes be seen in groups around a hummingbird feeder or in a flower garden. Ruby-throats are tough and feisty. They chase each other and try to keep other hummingbirds from getting any food. Hummingbirds can beat their wings in a figure-eight motion at 75 times a second, which allows them to hover in one place and even fly sideways and backwards. They burn so much energy that they need to eat all the time and can consume their body weight in food every day. When these birds are flying, their hearts beat an amazing 1,250 times per minute, compared to an active person's 100 to 120.

SCIENTIFIC NAME: *Archilochus colubris*
LENGTH: 3¾ in (10 cm)
WINGSPAN: 4½ in (11 cm)

VOICE

Hummingbirds aren't great singers, but they produce soft *tchew* notes and a surprisingly loud series of rapid squeals—*ch'ch'ch' ch'ch*—when chasing away a rival. When a hummingbird is nearby, you can hear a humming sound—like a buzzing bee—made by its rapidly beating wings.

FOOD

A hummingbird laps up nectar—its long tongue has a brushy tip that holds the sugary liquid and pulls it back into its mouth. These birds also eat tiny insects, which are the main food fed to baby hummingbirds. If you put up a hummingbird feeder, you'll get a really close look at these beautiful birds.

HABITAT & RANGE

Ruby-throats spend the spring and summer in parks, gardens, meadows, and along woodland edges across the eastern U.S. and Canada. In winter most fly to Mexico or Central America. The trip from the Texas coast to the Yucatán

A FEMALE Ruby-throated Hummingbird has a **white** throat and a glittering **green** back.

A CLOSER LOOK

Only the male has an iridescent, ruby-red throat (or *gorget*)—at some angles it looks black.

Very tiny legs and feet for perching—hummingbirds can't really walk.

Long bill for probing into flowers

Able to hover on rapidly beating wings

Blackish forked tail

Adult male

Peninsula in Mexico is about 500 miles (805 km), an amazing, nonstop journey for a bird that weighs less than a penny. Stored body fat is the fuel that powers its flight.

RANGE MAP KEY

SUMMER (breeding)	WINTER (nonbreeding)
MIGRATION	YEAR-ROUND

A THIMBLE-SIZE HOME

Made of dandelion down, tiny wisps of root and grass, and held together with strands of sticky spider's web, the tiny nest of a Ruby-throat is built by the female bird on top of a tree branch—construction takes about five days. She first makes a firm base and then builds up the one-inch (2.5-cm) walls, forming them between her neck and chest. The walls remain pliable and can stretch as the baby hummingbirds grow. As a final touch, the outside is decorated with flakes of lichen, which may help hide the nest from predators.

Blue Jay

LOUD, COLORFUL, BOSSY, intelligent, thieving, and bold are words that describe Blue Jays. But sometimes—while they are nesting in the summer—Blue Jays are shy and stay hidden. In fall, many jays migrate south in noisy bands, a pretty sight to see as they fly above the changing autumn leaves.

SCIENTIFIC NAME: *Cyanocitta cristata*
LENGTH: 11 in (28 cm)
WINGSPAN: 16 in (41 cm)

If you know where an oak tree grows, that is a great spot to look for a Blue Jay, who has a huge appetite for acorns. In fact, when there are too many acorns to eat, Blue Jays hide them throughout the forest, tucking them under leaves and into brush piles. Sometimes, they forget to retrieve an acorn, and it sprouts—a new oak tree begins life and will someday produce acorns to feed future generations of Blue Jays.

VOICE

All kinds of sounds come out of a Blue Jay's mouth, depending on what it's doing or how it's feeling. When making a fuss, it calls out a piercing *jay, jay, jay!* Quieter sounds include a soft *wheedle-wheedle* and a whistled *tooli*. It often mimics the loud screaming call of the Red-shouldered Hawk (see p. 30), so don't get fooled.

FOOD

Blue Jays—like people—are omnivores, that is, they eat lots of different foods: nuts, seeds, fruits, insects, worms, and even other birds' eggs and small animals like frogs or mice. Sometimes they search for food in the treetops, and sometimes they look on the ground. Blue Jays are more than happy to eat cracked corn, peanuts, or suet at a bird feeder, where they often chase smaller birds away until they have had their fill.

HABITAT & RANGE

If you live just about anywhere in the East, chances are you've seen this bird. It likes forests, especially oak forests, but is also quite content to live in a tree-filled

DURING CONFRONTATIONS Blue Jays try to look as **large** as possible.

A CLOSER LOOK

A large throat pouch (hidden) can expand to carry two or three acorns.

White spots on blue wings

Long tail feathers with white tips

Crest, sometimes flattened

Blackish necklace

city park or suburban backyard. Birds living in far northern areas migrate south in the fall, but, in most areas of the East, Blue Jays can be seen year-round.

RANGE MAP KEY

☐ SUMMER (breeding)   ☐ WINTER (nonbreeding)
☐ YEAR-ROUND

CHECK OUT MY CREST

Just as a frown or smile lets you know how a friend is feeling, the Blue Jay's crest signals to nearby birds if it is relaxed or mad. When the bird is sitting on its nest, feeding its nestlings, or just hanging out with its mate or family, its crest is flattened. When it is feeling threatened or aggressive, its crest is held up. The higher the crest, the more agitated the Blue Jay.

23

Black-capped Chickadee

CHICKADEES ARE ENERGETIC little birds that aren't very afraid of people. In fall and winter noisy little parties of chickadees join together with other species, such as titmice and nuthatches, and roam the woods looking for good food sources. Or they might spend the entire winter just hanging around your bird feeder. In summer, chickadees nest in tree cavities and birdhouses and become quieter and more secretive. South of where the Black-capped lives, it is replaced by the nearly identical Carolina Chickadee. Look for the state where you live on the range map (next page); if you live south of the states colored purple, you probably have Carolina Chickadees in your backyard.

SCIENTIFIC NAME: *Poecile atricapillus*
LENGTH: 5¼ in (13 cm)
WINGSPAN: 8 in (20 cm)

VOICE

All year-round, the friendly and trusting chickadee calls out its name *chick-a-dee-dee-dee*. In the spring and summer you can also hear its sweetly whistled song *fee bee* with the first note higher than the second.

FOOD

During the warmer months, chickadees poke into tree bark crevices and leaves for small flying insects and caterpillars. As winter approaches and insects get harder to find, they switch to eating seeds and berries.

HABITAT & RANGE

Black-capped Chickadees love trees of all sorts and are rarely found in wide-open areas. They nest in tree cavities, sometimes excavating their own hole in a rotted tree trunk or using an old woodpecker hole. Woodsy suburbs are excellent places for chickadees to live, and when people live nearby there is often the bonus of free food and lodging (bird feeders and birdhouses). Chickadees don't migrate. They live in the same place all year, although they may wander a bit in the winter.

PUT UP A BIRD FEEDER and get ready for action. **Chickadees** will probably be the first birds to discover your **bird feeder.**

A CLOSER LOOK

Black throat and cap

White cheeks

Gray back and wings

Jerky flight; usually flies only short distances between trees

Buffy sides, brighter in winter

RANGE MAP KEY

WINTER (nonbreeding)

YEAR-ROUND

A BIRD IN THE HAND

Do you have what it takes to make friends with a chickadee ... and have it perch on your hand? Try this. Walk slowly to a spot near your bird feeder and stand very still with some sunflower seeds in your extended hand. Don't make any quick movements. It might take several tries over a few days, but chickadees will start to trust you as they get to know you. Wear the same hat and coat so they recognize you as a friend.

American Robin

WHEN THE EARLY COLONISTS arrived in North America they saw a bird that reminded them of a common bird from back home in Europe, so they gave it the same name: Robin. The name stuck, even though our American Robin is a member of the thrush family and isn't related to the European Robin. The American Robin, common all across the U.S., is easy to recognize with its reddish breast, upright stance, and potbellied look. Watch a robin make its way across a grassy lawn in search of something squirmy to eat. It moves in a jerky run-stop-run pattern, then stops and cocks its head to look for an earthworm or grub. After a long winter, a sure sign that spring has arrived is the male robin singing his loud song.

SCIENTIFIC NAME: *Turdus migratorius*
LENGTH: 10 in (25 cm)
WINGSPAN: 17 in (43 cm)

VITAL STATISTICS

VOICE

The male robin's loud and lively song has a bubbly quality. It's made up of short phrases: *cheerily-cheer up-cheerio*. Males and females both give soft clucking calls and a variety of shrill alarm calls.

FOOD

Robins eat earthworms, but that's not all. Robins also poke around under fallen leaves in search of insects. During the winter, most robins switch to a diet of fruits and berries. You can often see groups of robins feeding in holly trees and other plants with red berries. After the berries are gone, the flock moves on to a different location.

HABITAT & RANGE

Robins are widespread and common, so you should be able to see them wherever you live in North America. They are found in a variety of wooded areas, open fields, and urban and suburban areas. In summer, they nest as far north as Alaska, almost to the Arctic Ocean. Most robins migrate in a southern direction, sometimes

A YOUNG ROBIN has a heavily **spotted** breast.

A CLOSER LOOK

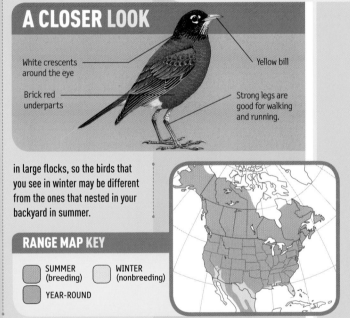

White crescents around the eye

Brick red underparts

Yellow bill

Strong legs are good for walking and running.

in large flocks, so the birds that you see in winter may be different from the ones that nested in your backyard in summer.

RANGE MAP KEY

- SUMMER (breeding)
- WINTER (nonbreeding)
- YEAR-ROUND

HOME SWEET HOME

Some sturdy sticks, a little dried grass, all glued together with some sticky mud—it's a bit untidy, but a robin's nest is just temporary housing. After construction, the female lays four blue eggs and sits on them (incubates them) for 12 to 14 days until they hatch. The baby robins grow quickly and leave the nest after about two weeks, never to return. Robins aren't shy around people, and sometimes they even nest under a porch roof or on a protected windowsill.

27

Northern Cardinal

THE BRIGHT RED male Northern Cardinal ("redbird") might be America's most popular bird. Because of its colorful plumage and stylish good looks, the cardinal is the official state bird of seven states—Illinois, Indiana, Kentucky, North Carolina, Ohio, Virginia, and West Virginia—more than any other species. People often think that every bright red bird they see is a cardinal, even though some tanagers and finches are equally red. If you want to know for sure, look for the cardinal's crest and massive red bill. Cardinals used to be seen mostly in the American South, but they have expanded their range far to the north and west since the 19th century because of changes in habitat and warming temperatures.

SCIENTIFIC NAME: *Cardinalis cardinalis*
LENGTH: 8¾ in (22 cm)
WINGSPAN: 12 in (30 cm)

VOICE

Unlike many other birds, male and female cardinals both sing, sometimes in a duet. They have a variety of songs, but a loud whistled *what-cheer! what-cheer! what-cheer!* or *purty-purty-purty* are common. Their call note is a sharp *pik*.

FOOD

Cardinals eat different foods at different times of the year. In spring and summer, their food is mostly insects with some flower buds, berries, and weed seeds mixed in. In winter, their favorite foods are seeds and some berries. A bird feeder stocked with black-oil sunflower seeds is sure to attract any cardinals living in your neighborhood.

HABITAT & RANGE

Cardinals are widespread and common in the East and Midwest, and abundant in the southern U.S. They like brushy habitats like woodland edges, thickets, vine tangles, shrubby backyards, and city parks. Surprisingly, Northern

A BABY Northern Cardinal may **leave** its nest before being able to fly. Its **parents** will follow it around and feed it.

A CLOSER LOOK

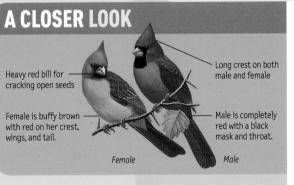

Heavy red bill for cracking open seeds

Long crest on both male and female

Female is buffy brown with red on her crest, wings, and tail.

Male is completely red with a black mask and throat.

Female

Male

Cardinals also live in the desert Southwest in dense shrubs and along riverbeds. These birds do not migrate. Instead they live in the same place all year long.

RANGE MAP KEY

YEAR-ROUND

WHAT THE HECK?

In the spring the feisty male Northern Cardinal, like most birds, establishes his nesting territory and defends it from others of his own species. Unfortunately, evolution has not taught him about reflections. A male cardinal will attack his own reflection in a car mirror thinking it is another bird moving in on his space.

Mini-Profiles
EASTERN BACKYARD

Here are 12 more species of birds that live in eastern backyards. Many of these birds love to eat seeds from a bird feeder or scattered on the ground.

MOURNING DOVE

SCIENTIFIC NAME: *Zenaida macroura*
LENGTH: 12 in (31 cm)
WINGSPAN: 18 in (46 cm)

There are the same number of Mourning Doves living in the U.S. as there are people —about 350 million. They live in open areas including suburban yards. Listen for the dove's slow, mournful call, *oowoo-woo-woo-woo*, and the whistling sound made by its wings when it bursts into flight. You can attract doves to your backyard by scattering birdseed on the ground.

RED-SHOULDERED HAWK

SCIENTIFIC NAME: *Buteo lineatus*
LENGTH: 17 in (43 cm)
WINGSPAN: 40 in (102 cm)

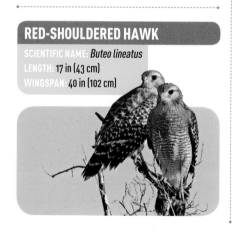

The colorful Red-shouldered Hawk is a very vocal bird with a loud screaming call, *KEE-ahh*. When you hear its call, look up to see it soaring over wooded backyards. To catch its prey, the hawk perches quietly at the edge of the woods and then pounces down on small mammals and reptiles.

DOWNY WOODPECKER

SCIENTIFIC NAME: *Picoides pubescens*
LENGTH: 6¾ in (17 cm)
WINGSPAN: 12 in (30 cm)

The tiny Downy Woodpecker—the smallest woodpecker in North America—is common across the continent from Maine to California. The Downy is the woodpecker most likely to show up at a bird feeder, where it prefers to eat suet (animal fat, usually mixed with seeds or fruit). Like most woodpeckers, it is black and white, although the male has a spot of bright red on the back of his head. This bird is small enough to search for food on thin branches and weed stems that couldn't support its larger, similar-looking cousin, the Hairy Woodpecker. The Downy's call is a sharp, high-pitched *pik!*

EASTERN PHOEBE

SCIENTIFIC NAME: *Sayornis phoebe*
LENGTH: 7 in (18 cm)
WINGSPAN: 10½ in (27 cm)

From spring through fall this medium-size flycatcher is often seen around houses, barns, and sheds. You might hear it call out its name, *fee-bee*, before you see it. Phoebes like to nest in sheltered locations and often choose an open porch if it has a ledge that will support its nest. The Eastern Phoebe returns to its northern breeding locations early in the spring. Its body is dark brown above and whitish below. Even when perched, it doesn't stay still—it constantly pumps its tail up and down.

WHITE-BREASTED NUTHATCH

SCIENTIFIC NAME: *Sitta carolinensis*
LENGTH: 5¾ in (15 cm)
WINGSPAN: 11 in (28 cm)

If you see a small gray-and-white bird climbing nimbly up, down, and around a tree trunk, chances are good that you've spotted a White-breasted Nuthatch. The nuthatch has an extra-long hind claw that helps it get a grip in any position. It lives year-round in woods and wooded backyards and is crazy about suet feeders. Its call is a low-pitched nasal *yank*.

CAROLINA WREN

SCIENTIFIC NAME: *Thryothorus ludovicianus*
LENGTH: 5¼ in (13 cm)
WINGSPAN: 7½ in (19 cm)

The Carolina Wren is small and chunky, with a long tail and long bill curved downward. Its plumage is a buffy orange below and reddish brown above with a bold white eye stripe. The Carolina Wren has lots of personality. If you leave a back porch door open for a few hours, a Carolina Wren will probably poke inside for a look. When not poking around where people live, it searches in shrubs, brush piles, and berry patches for insects and spiders. The male is a masterful singer and may sing dozens of different song variations.

GRAY CATBIRD

SCIENTIFIC NAME: *Dumetella carolinensis*
LENGTH: 8½ in (22 cm)
WINGSPAN: 11 in (28 cm)

The Gray Catbird is well named—it's mostly gray and gives a call that sounds like the raspy mew of a cat. If you get a good look, you'll see a patch of rusty red under its tail. In spring and early summer, the male catbird strings together a series of short songs into a long song that can last for minutes. Some parts of his song are imitations of other birds, insects, frogs, and even car noises. The song is used to defend his nesting territory and to warn other catbirds to keep out. Catbirds nest in low shrubs and rarely perch high in a tree or venture out in the open for long. In summer they eat mostly insects, but also consume small fruits such as poison ivy berries, grapes, and blackberries.

AMERICAN GOLDFINCH

SCIENTIFIC NAME: *Spinus tristis*
LENGTH: 5 in (13 cm)
WINGSPAN: 9 in (23 cm)

From spring to fall, male goldfinches have dazzling yellow plumage and a black cap and wings. In the winter, males are a more subdued tan color, as are the females year-round. Goldfinches are common in overgrown fields, backyards, and along roadsides across the continent, and they like to visit bird feeders. The goldfinch is the state bird of Iowa, New Jersey, and Washington. Its flight call *per-chik-o-ree* sounds like "po-ta-to chip."

CHIPPING SPARROW

SCIENTIFIC NAME: *Spizella passerina*
LENGTH: 5½ in (14 cm)
WINGSPAN: 8½ in (22 cm)

This pretty little sparrow wears a rusty red cap in spring and summer that makes it easy to identify. Chipping Sparrows are common across North America in areas with trees and grassy openings—like many backyards. Although they perch and nest in trees, Chipping Sparrows find most of their food on the ground. The food consists mostly of small seeds and insects, some of which are pursued through the air. The male Chipping Sparrow's territorial song is a long mechanical-sounding trill of dry *chip* notes. He is a persistent singer and in spring and summer his monotonous song can be heard all day long. In fall, Chipping Sparrows migrate to warmer southern U.S. states or into Mexico.

WHITE-THROATED SPARROW

SCIENTIFIC NAME: *Zonotrichia albicollis*
LENGTH: 6¾ in (17 cm)
WINGSPAN: 9 in (23 cm)

In the spring, these sparrows travel to northern areas to breed, but in the winter they are very common around backyards and forest edges. Feed them by scattering seed on the ground and you might get a large flock hanging around all winter. Take a close look and you'll see that some sparrows have black-and-white head stripes (the hardcore aggressive birds) and others have tan-and-white stripes (the laid-back passive birds). This has nothing to do with being male or female, and successful breeding pairs usually consist of one of each type. Its song sounds like "Old Sam Peabody, Peabody, Peabody."

DARK-EYED JUNCO

SCIENTIFIC NAME: *Junco hyemalis*
LENGTH: 6¼ in (16 cm)
WINGSPAN: 9½ in (24 cm)

Although the junco that lives in the East is a small gray-and-white bird, it has some flash—its dazzling white tail feathers. When hopping around on the ground and when taking flight, the white outer tail feathers make it easy to identify. That flash of white may warn other juncos of danger. Little flocks of these dapper sparrows—known to many as "snowbirds"—show up at backyard feeders as winter weather is about to set in. Juncos are also summer breeding birds in New England and in the Appalachian Mountains. The junco's plumage varies geographically—more than any other American sparrow. The birds out West look quite different.

BALTIMORE ORIOLE

SCIENTIFIC NAME: *Icterus galbula*
LENGTH: 8¼ in (21 cm)
WINGSPAN: 11½ in (29 cm)

A flash of orange in the top of a large shade tree, the sound of loud, flute-like whistles, or the sight of a woven nest drooping from the tip of a high branch are all signs that a pair of Baltimore Orioles are living nearby. Seen through a pair of binoculars, the male is a tropical-looking fireball of orange and black, and the female is only slightly less colorful. The Baltimore Oriole is the official state bird of Maryland, which is, of course, also the home of the Baltimore Orioles baseball team.

ANNA'S HUMMINGBIRD

Western
Backyard
Birds

Western Backyard

HABITAT

ANNA'S HUMMINGBIRD

ACORN WOODPECKER

A TREASURE TROVE OF BIRDS!

The western states of California, Oregon, and Washington, and the Canadian province of British Columbia are chock-full of amazing birds. In this chapter you'll get to know 17 bird species that live all over the West and show up in backyards. Whether you live in San Diego, California, or Seattle, Washington, you have a good chance of seeing all or most of them. Keep your eyes open and you'll see lots of other birds too, especially if you can put up a bird feeder.

BULLOCK'S ORIOLE

NORTHERN MOCKINGBIRD

CALIFORNIA SCRUB-JAY

Anna's Hummingbird

ANNA'S HUMMINGBIRDS are the most common hummingbirds along the Pacific coast. Backyard gardens with lots of flowers and a hummingbird feeder are a magnet for them. Most male hummingbirds have a shining jewel-like throat, but the male Anna's has even more bling—the top of his head glows rose red like his throat. When the sun hits it just right, it's like a magical ruby spotlight was turned on. Then, with a shift of his head, the light goes off and the feathers look black. (The way the color and light is created is called iridescence.) Native Americans revered hummingbirds and had many legends about them. One story describes how the hummingbird used its sharp, pointed bill to poke holes in the black sky and created stars.

SCIENTIFIC NAME: *Calypte anna*
LENGTH: 4 in (10 cm)
WINGSPAN: 5¼ in (13 cm)

VOICE

The male Anna's Hummingbird carries a pretty good tune, but to human ears it sounds more like a jumble of high-pitched squeaks and scratchy notes. The male and female give high, sharp calls *chit, chit, chid-it, chit*. When they are chasing away rival hummingbirds, listen for a rapid series of rattle-like calls *jika, jika, jika*.

FOOD

Like the Ruby-throat (see pp. 20–21), these humming-birds use their long tongue to lap up nectar from flowers. They also eat tiny insects, which are the main food fed to baby hummingbirds. You might see a hummingbird poking into shallow holes in a tree trunk that were made by a woodpecker—it's feeding on the sugary tree sap and any insects attracted to it.

HABITAT & RANGE

One hundred years ago Anna's Hummingbirds lived only in southern California and northern Baja California (in Mexico). Today their range extends north to Canada. What changed? People planted gardens of

FEMALES build nests and care for **babies** without help from males.

A CLOSER LOOK

Only the male has an iridescent red throat and crown—at some angles it looks black (females have a few red feathers on their throats).

Adult male

Young males have patchy red throats.

Zooms around backyards on buzzing wings

exotic flowering plants and trees, and the hummingbirds followed. In the warm climate, the birds can find flower nectar even in winter, so they don't migrate.

RANGE MAP KEY

- SUMMER (breeding)
- WINTER (nonbreeding)
- YEAR-ROUND

CHOOSE ME!

To impress a female Anna's Hummingbird, the male has an awesome display flight. You might even see one in your backyard. It starts with the male hum-mingbird hovering in front of the female, and then flying straight up to over 100 feet (30.5 m). From there he plummets in a high-speed dive to within inches of the perched female, making a loud *PEEK!* sound with his tail feathers as he pulls out of the dive. The performance finishes with a "shuttle display" as he flies back and forth a foot (30 cm) above the female, while singing his squeaky love song. Sometimes a charged-up male will even display to a nearby person.

Acorn Woodpecker

ACORN WOODPECKERS are great fun to watch. They love company, living in colonies of a dozen or more related birds that might include aunts, uncles, brothers, sisters, and, of course, mom and dad. They all work together to gather and store thousands of acorns in a special storage tree (granary tree) so that the colony will have food in the winter months. The granary tree is the center of the colony and it's not unusual for groups of birds to gather there, calling loudly and flashing their wings in a woodpecker greeting. The birds also share other chores and responsibilities. One-year-old birds don't breed, but they stay with the colony and help raise the baby birds by feeding and caring for them.

SCIENTIFIC NAME: *Melanerpes formicivorus*
LENGTH: 9¼ in (24 cm)
WINGSPAN: 17½ in (44 cm)

VITAL STATISTICS

VOICE

Very noisy! Acorn Woodpeckers don't sing, but they loudly call *wakka-wakka-wakka* or *ja-cob, ja-cob, ja-cob.* Sometimes groups gather on a tree limb and call back and forth while spreading their flashy wings. The zany calls of the Acorn Woodpecker inspired Walter Lantz to create the famous cartoon character Woody Woodpecker.

FOOD

Obviously, Acorn Woodpeckers have a taste for acorns, but they eat other things as well. On warm days they catch flying insects by spying them from a high perch and snatching them in flight (flycatching). Wild fruit and tree sap are also on their diet.

HABITAT & RANGE

Look for these western birds wherever oak trees occur, in mountain forests, backyards, and even city parks. If they're around, these noisy birds are hard to miss. A colony of Acorn Woodpeckers

defends its feeding territory—usually a grove of oak trees—and lives in the same place year-round. The only reason they might wander is if they can't find food.

IN FLIGHT or when calling, the Acorn Woodpecker flashes the **white** feathers in its wings and on its rump.

A CLOSER LOOK

Female

Clownlike face pattern and white eyes

Male

Stiff, black tail feathers, used for support when clinging to a tree trunk

Glossy black back with white patches in the wings and on the rump

RANGE MAP KEY

☐ YEAR-ROUND

ONE FOR ALL AND ALL FOR ONE

The members of an Acorn Woodpecker colony spend lots of time storing acorns by drilling holes that exactly fit the acorns. A single tree (known as a granary tree) may have thousands and thousands of stored acorns for all the birds in the colony to share. Backyard Acorn Woodpeckers sometimes choose a telephone pole or even the side of a wooden house to drill into. If a squirrel, jay, or woodpecker from a different colony tries to steal acorns from them, the whole colony drives the thief away with lots of loud calls and swooping attacks.

California Scrub-Jay

CALIFORNIA SCRUB-JAYS ARE very smart birds, like their relatives the crows and ravens. They always seem to be figuring out an angle that will score them an easy meal or some kind of advantage. They're not above stealing food from other birds that they can intimidate or outwit. Sometimes a jay will spy on another jay that has some food it is trying to hide. Afterward, it sneaks in and takes the food from the other bird's hiding place. When they are stashing food away, most jays learn to look around first and make sure that they aren't being spied on. When a predator, such as a snake or owl, is spotted, a jay will shriek for minutes at a time, warning others about the danger.

SCIENTIFIC NAME: *Aphelocoma californica*
LENGTH: 11 in (28 cm)
WINGSPAN: 15½ in (39 cm)

VOICE

Although not a musical singer, the California Scrub-Jay's calls are very loud and attract a lot of attention. The most common call is a harsh, up-slurred *jaaay?* or *jreeee?* that sounds like a question being asked. When jays are in flight or upset about something, you might hear a noisy series of *shee-yuk, shee-yuk, shee-yuk* calls.

FOOD

Like the Blue Jay that lives in the East, the California Scrub-Jay eats a variety of foods, usually whatever is easiest to find or capture. Sometimes the meal is vegetarian (seeds, nuts, fruit) and other times it's animal (insects, small lizards, bird's eggs). Scrub-Jays are also frequent visitors to bird feeders, where they especially like peanuts and sunflower seeds.

HABITAT & RANGE

California Scrub-Jays are found in many different places. In the wild, they live in oak woodlands or brushy areas, but they are very adaptable and are quite happy to live in a backyard or a city park. They don't migrate. A pair—male and female—stays together

SCRUB-JAYS often **chase** smaller birds away from a feeder.

A CLOSER LOOK

Azure blue head with a white eyebrow

Heavy, black bill is an all-purpose tool.

Mostly blue above with a blue breast band

Rounded head, similar to the Steller's Jay, which also lives in the West, but has a tall crest

Short wings and long tail make it easy to fly in tight places.

throughout the year. During the nesting season they will chase off other jays that might try to move into their home territory. In the winter they're friendlier to each other and sometimes hang out together in flocks.

RANGE MAP KEY

YEAR-ROUND

HIDE-AND-SEEK

Did you ever hide something and then forget where you put it? That hardly ever happens to a California Scrub-Jay. When acorns or pine nuts are abundant, a jay will hide hundreds of them—under a rock, in a bark crevice, behind some twigs, almost anywhere. Amazingly, the jay—unlike a human—will remember where almost all of them are stashed, even months later. Scientists aren't sure how the birds do it.

Northern Mockingbird

HAVE YOU EVER HEARD a bird singing late at night? If you answer yes, you probably have a Northern Mockingbird living in your neighborhood. A male mockingbird sometimes sings all night long, trying to attract attention from a female. This songbird is truly an awe-inspiring singer, "sampling" the songs of many other birds into his own creation. He will repeat each song snippet three or more times and then move on to a different one. A single mockingbird can sing hundreds of different song fragments. Females sing too, although they do it more quietly and less often. Mockingbirds (and all wild birds) are protected, so it's against the law to keep them as pets, but you can enjoy them singing in your backyard.

SCIENTIFIC NAME: *Mimus polyglottos*
LENGTH: 10 in (25 cm)
WINGSPAN: 14 in (36 cm)

VOICE

Males and females both sing. The mockingbird adds the songs of many other birds into his performance (mimicry). Most of the long-winded song is composed of pleasant whistles, but the mockingbird adds in harsh scolds and trills. When chasing a rival away from a thicket full of berries, an angry mockingbird calls out a high raspy *skeeh, skeeh, skeeh*.

FOOD

The mockingbird eats a full menu of insects in spring and summer. Winter food is mostly berries, and many mockingbirds claim a favorite berry patch and chase off all other birds that get too close.

HABITAT & RANGE

Northern Mockingbirds are common from east to west, but they avoid colder areas like Canada and the northern states. They prefer to live in hedges and thickets with nearby open areas or lawns. Big backyards and overgrown fields are perfect, but they also live around suburban housing tracts and city parks with ornamental trees and shrubs. Most mockingbirds live in the same place all year long.

YOUNG mockingbirds look different from their parents; they have dark eyes and **spotted** breasts.

A CLOSER LOOK

Adults have yellow eyes.

White patches in the dark wings and tail (best seen in flight)

Adult

Males and females look the same.

Gray and white feathers

Juvenile

RANGE MAP KEY

- SUMMER (breeding)
- WINTER (nonbreeding)
- YEAR-ROUND

A FLASH OF WHITE

When a Northern Mockingbird is on the ground searching for a meal in the grass, you might see it stop suddenly and flash its wings open in a series of jerks—showing off its big white wing patches. Scientists aren't sure why the mockingbird does this so often; maybe it startles any insects hiding in the grass and makes it easier to catch them. Or, it might be a signal to other mockingbirds to stay away.

Bullock's Oriole

ORIOLES ARE THE "GOLDEN BIRDS" of the bird world. You might know that the Spanish word for "gold" is oro, the beginning of the word oriole. There are many species of orioles in North and South America, and most of them have golden yellow or orange colors in their plumage. The male Bullock's Oriole is dressed in a mixture of golden orange, black, and white. The female is less colorful, but has a golden yellow head and throat. A long time ago this oriole and its eastern cousin, the Baltimore Oriole (p. 33) were considered the same species, even though they look different. Scientists thought they were the same because their ranges overlap on the Great Plains.

SCIENTIFIC NAME: *Icterus bullockii*
LENGTH: 8¼ in (21 cm)
WINGSPAN: 12 in (30 cm)

VOICE

Unlike many songbirds, male and female Bullock's Orioles both sing, although males sing more often. Their song is a musical series of whistles ending in a sweeter note: kip, kit-tick, kit-tick, whew, wheet. Their rattle call is a harsh-sounding *cha-cha-cha-cha*, and is given as a warning or alarm.

FOOD

The Bullock's Oriole eats insects of all types. Orioles will come to special bird feeders that dispense jelly or nectar and are also attracted to oranges cut in half.

HABITAT & RANGE

The Bullock's Oriole breeds west of the Mississippi River. It seeks out large shade trees to nest in, especially sycamores and cotton-woods. Suburbs, ranches, golf courses, and even city parks are acceptable as long as there are tall trees that are not too close together. Deep forests and high mountains are avoided. Bullock's Orioles are migratory and after

ORIOLES will often feed on an **orange** that is cut in half.

A CLOSER LOOK

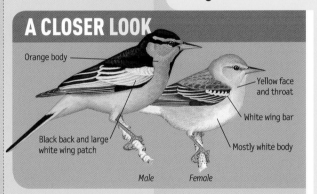

Orange body

Black back and large white wing patch

Yellow face and throat

White wing bar

Mostly white body

Male   *Female*

nesting, almost all of them leave the U.S. for their winter homes in Mexico and Guatemala.

RANGE MAP KEY

- SUMMER (breeding)
- WINTER (nonbreeding)
- MIGRATION
- YEAR-ROUND

ROCK-A-BYE BABY ...

Swaying in the breeze like a hammock, this oriole's nest is a neatly woven construction worthy of a master builder. It is located high in a large shade tree and often suspended from a few thin branches. Since it rocks in the wind and must support as many as five or six baby birds, it has to be strong. The female is in charge of the weaving although the male sometimes assists her.

Mini-Profiles

WESTERN BACKYARD

Many birds don't need wilderness places to live in—they do just fine with people for neighbors. Here are 12 more western backyard birds that you can look for.

RUFOUS HUMMINGBIRD

SCIENTIFIC NAME: *Selasphorus rufus*
LENGTH: 3½ in (9 cm)
WINGSPAN: 4½ in (11 cm)

The Rufous Hummingbird is a feisty species that breeds farther north than any other hummingbird, as far as Alaska. It is a common nesting bird in Oregon, Washington, and the Canadian province of British Columbia. The adult male has a flame-red throat (gorget). The female has a green back, some rufous on the tail and sides, and a mostly white throat. Rufous Hummingbirds spend the winter months in Mexico.

COOPER'S HAWK

SCIENTIFIC NAME: *Accipiter cooperii*
LENGTH: 17 in (43 cm)
WINGSPAN: 32 in (81 cm)

The Cooper's Hawk survives by hunting and eating smaller birds. Backyards with bird feeders are often visited by a Cooper's Hawk looking to ambush a distracted bird. In the air, its long tail works like a rudder, so it can turn on a dime. And its supersharp talons easily grab a flying bird. If a particular hawk bothers your bird feeder too often, take the feeder down for a few days until the hawk moves on.

BLACK PHOEBE

SCIENTIFIC NAME: *Sayornis nigricans*
LENGTH: 6¾ in (17 cm)
WINGSPAN: 11 in (28 cm)

The only black-and-white flycatcher in North America, the Black Phoebe is elegantly dressed in what resembles a black shirt and white pants. Active and trusting, this little bird darts out to catch flying insects and scarcely notices people nearby. Black Phoebes are often seen in places where there is water, like a wild stream or lake, as well as around backyard swimming pools and park fountains.

BUSHTIT

SCIENTIFIC NAME: *Psaltriparus minimus*
LENGTH: 4½ in (13 cm)
WINGSPAN: 8 in (20 cm)

Yes, Bushtit really is its common name! You hardly ever see just one Bushtit; they live in small flocks of 10 to 40 birds that stay close together all year. They are tiny, mostly gray birds with a ball-shaped body and a long tail, and are a common resident of backyard gardens and parks as well as wilder places. The Bushtit's nest is a remarkable hanging home that is woven of plant fibers and spiderwebs and then decorated with bits of other plants to keep it hidden (camouflaged). It may take more than a month to build.

HOUSE WREN

SCIENTIFIC NAME: *Troglodytes aedon*
LENGTH: 4¾ in (12 cm)
WINGSPAN: 6 in (15 cm)

The male House Wren's loud and bubbly song is a familiar summer sound in backyards across North America. The song is sung from an exposed perch and delivered with such force that his whole body quivers with the effort. His message is, "Keep out, this is my territory!" House Wrens are small brown birds without much pattern. They prefer shrubby edges and open woods and spend most of their time low to the ground, where they search for insects and spiders to eat. For nesting, they choose small cavities, such as old woodpecker holes, rock crevices, and birdhouses. As winter approaches, they migrate south to warmer areas.

HOUSE FINCH

SCIENTIFIC NAME: *Haemorhous mexicanus*
LENGTH: 6 in (15 cm)
WINGSPAN: 9½ in (24 cm)

At one time, House Finches lived only in the West. After some caged House Finches were released on Long Island in 1940, they eventually spread throughout the United States. They eat seeds and have a thick bill for cracking them open. The male has a bright red head and breast. The female has streaky brown plumage that is good camouflage when she is sitting on her nest.

LESSER GOLDFINCH

SCIENTIFIC NAME: *Spinus psaltria*
LENGTH: 4½ in (11 cm)
WINGSPAN: 8 in (20 cm)

The Lesser Goldfinch is the slightly smaller cousin of the American Goldfinch (p. 32). In California and nearby states, Lesser Goldfinch males have black caps and green backs, but males farther east have black backs. Both males and females have yellow underparts. Goldfinches eat a mostly vegetarian diet of seeds, tiny fruits, and plant buds, and very occasionally a small insect. Being a small bird, its nest is about the size of a tennis ball cut in half, and holds three to six eggs. Cottonwoods and willows are favorite nesting sites. In many places they are year-round residents, but in colder northern areas, they move south in the fall.

CALIFORNIA TOWHEE

SCIENTIFIC NAME: *Melozone crissalis*
LENGTH: 9 in (23 cm)
WINGSPAN: 11½ in (29 cm)

The California Towhee is sort of drab-looking—mostly brown with a little rusty orange color under its tail—and it rarely moves far from where it nests. It's a type of large sparrow, and if you live in California there's a good chance there's a pair living in your neighborhood. Pairs stay together all year and often call back and forth *chink, chink, chink* to each other as they scratch at the ground hunting for seeds or insects hidden under fallen leaves. They also like to eat birdseed and cracked corn scattered on the ground.

SPOTTED TOWHEE

SCIENTIFIC NAME: *Pipilo maculatus*
LENGTH: 8½ in (22 cm)
WINGSPAN: 10½ in (27 cm)

Towhees are very large sparrows. The Spotted Towhee's plumage is a complicated patchwork of black, white, brown, and rufous (reddish brown). In flight its long tail has very noticeable white tips. Its close relative, the Eastern Towhee, is very similar, but lacks white spots on its back. Spotted Towhees specialize in hunting for food under fallen leaves. To move the leaves aside they use both feet at once to kick the leaves backward. Since it is often hidden out of sight under shrubbery, you might hear a Spotted Towhee rustling around in the dead leaves before you see it. These towhees will visit a platform bird feeder if it is located near the ground.

WHITE-CROWNED SPARROW

SCIENTIFIC NAME: *Zonotrichia leucophrys*
LENGTH: 7 in (18 cm)
WINGSPAN: 9½ in (24 cm)

In many places this attractive "crowned" sparrow is best known as a winter visitor to backyards—especially along the West Coast, where it is abundant. The black-and-white head stripes of adults are hard to miss. Young birds have brown-and-white stripes. Unlike many birds, the White-crowned sings all winter long. Its song is made up of mournful whistles, followed by jumbled notes and ending in a buzz or trill. Some birds live year-round along the West Coast, but most birds seen in western backyards nest far to the north, in the Canadian tundra. A backyard bird feeder will coax them into the open for a good look.

BLACK-HEADED GROSBEAK

SCIENTIFIC NAME: *Pheucticus melanocephalus*
LENGTH: 8¼ in (21 cm)
WINGSPAN: 12½ in (32 cm)

The Black-headed Grosbeak is a chunky, colorful songbird with a large bill. The male is striking with a cinnamon orange chest that contrasts with his black head and boldly patterned wings. Females are more subtly marked with brown, yellow-brown, and white. The male's song is a series of singsong phrases. The call of both males and females is a sharp *pik* that sounds like a squeaky door. It eats a diet of insects, seeds, buds, and fruit, and will visit bird feeders that offer sunflower seeds. In fall, the entire population migrates to Mexico and spends the winter there.

BREWER'S BLACKBIRD

SCIENTIFIC NAME: *Euphagus cyanocephalus*
LENGTH: 9 in (23 cm)
WINGSPAN: 15 in (38 cm)

Brewer's Blackbirds are survivors and have actually become more common across most of North America in places where people live and farm. They do well in backyards and along city streets, where you might find a small flock looking for fallen food scraps under the tables of an outdoor restaurant. Although they look simply black most of the time, when the full sun reflects off the male's glossy plumage you'll see the most beautiful combination of metallic green, rich purple, and deep blue.

City

Streets and Parks

HOUSE SPARROW

City Streets and Parks

HABITAT

HOUSE SPARROW

EUROPEAN STARLING

STREET LIFE

City streets might not look like a place where any birds would want to live. How does a bird find a meal or raise a nestful of baby birds in a big city? In fact, for some birds the city is an ideal place. There is a population boom among the bird species that can meet the challenges of street life in our cities. If you live in a city near a park with trees and a pond, you'll see even more species.

PEREGRINE FALCON

ROCK PIGEON

RING-BILLED GULL

55

Peregrine Falcon

SCIENTIFIC NAME: *Falco peregrinus*
LENGTH: 17 in (43 cm)
WINGSPAN: 41 in (104 cm)

THE PEREGRINE FALCON WOULD be an Olympic gold medalist in the bird world. It holds the world record for speed among birds—over 200 miles an hour (322 km/h). This speedy bird eats other birds. It attacks its prey by dropping down from high above in a spectacular high-speed dive called a stoop. With its large, powerful feet, the Peregrine hits its prey, stunning or killing it, and then grabs it before it hits the ground. In the wild, Peregrines breed where there are cliffs for nesting, but in recent years many have taken up the city life. Ledges on tall skyscrapers, water towers, and bridges take the place of cliffs, and there are plenty of city pigeons to feed on.

VOICE

Falcons are usually silent. Around their nest they give a rapid series of harsh calls—*kak-kak-kak*—when upset or communicating with their young.

FOOD

Peregrine Falcons eat mostly birds, caught and killed in flight and then taken to a perch to be plucked and eaten. In North America, over 450 different species have been documented as prey, from tiny hummingbirds to giant Sandhill Cranes, but most are medium-size birds like ducks, sandpipers, and pigeons. Peregrines also hunt bats if they are available and sometimes steal the prey of other raptors.

HABITAT & RANGE

Peregrine Falcons were almost extinct in eastern North America about 50 years ago because of a pesticide called DDT that got into their bodies. When DDT was banned in 1972, the falcons started to recover and now are no longer endangered. Peregrine Falcons live in many places from coastal cities to high mountains and occur on every continent except Antarctica. The name

YOUNG PEREGRINES (juveniles) are **browner** than their parents and are streaked underneath. This one lives on the side of a **skyscraper.**

A CLOSER LOOK

Juvenile

Blue-gray above with a blackish hood

Black wedge of feathers below the eye helps reduce the sun's glare, just like the black face paint used by some football and baseball players.

Adult

Large feet with sharp talons to grasp prey

Hooked bill for plucking feathers and tearing flesh

Pointed wings are built for speed.

Long tail makes quick, high-speed turns possible.

"peregrine" means wanderer, and some Peregrine Falcons that nest in the Arctic wander as far as South America during the winter months.

RANGE MAP KEY

- SUMMER (breeding)
- WINTER (nonbreeding)
- MIGRATION
- YEAR-ROUND

FALCONRY—THE SPORT OF KINGS

People have trained falcons for hunting for over 2,000 years. Many different types of hawks and falcons have been used, but the Peregrine and its larger relative the Gyrfalcon have always been the most prized. In early times these birds were reserved for the use of royalty. Today most falcons used for hunting were hatched in captivity, and owning one requires a special permit. Training a young falcon to hunt and come back to its owner takes months of dedicated work. At some airports, trained falcons are used to scare off flocks of birds that might collide with an airplane.

Ring-billed Gull

RING-BILLED GULLS are medium-size gulls. Adults have a white head and a yellow bill with a black ring around it. It takes about two and a half years for a baby Ring-bill to become an adult. During that time its plumage is speckled with brown, and its bill is pinkish with a black tip. This gull was nearly wiped out between 1860 and 1920. Today there may be as many as eight million Ring-billed Gulls living in North America, and their population is growing. They have become a nuisance around some city airports where a collision with an airplane can be dangerous to the airplane (and the gull). Some airports hire falconers and their tame falcons to scare the gulls away.

SCIENTIFIC NAME: *Larus delawarensis*
LENGTH: 12½ in (32 cm)
WINGSPAN: 28 in (71 cm)

VOICE

Ring-billed Gulls make a variety of sounds. None of them are sweet-sounding songs. As a bird is landing it sounds off with a loud *kyow*.

FOOD

The Ring-billed Gull is not a picky eater. Scientists call it an opportunistic feeder—its favorite food is whatever is right in front of it.

HABITAT & RANGE

When hanging out in city parks and around dumpsters these so-called "sea gulls" look out of place to many people who may expect to see them only at the beach. Some gull species live all over the place, not just at the beach. That's why birders simply call them gulls. During breeding season, Ring-billed Gulls move to inland lakes and waterways and usually nest on uninhabited islands. Nesting on an island is often safer than other places because it is less likely to have predators such as foxes, skunks, and raccoons.

YOUNG **Ring-billed Gulls** have plumage with brown streaks.

A CLOSER LOOK

Yellow eyes and legs — White head and underparts

Yellow bill with a black "ring" — Black wing tip

Pale gray upperparts

RANGE MAP KEY

- SUMMER (breeding)
- WINTER (nonbreeding)
- MIGRATION
- YEAR-ROUND

THE DAILY GRIND

Have you ever seen flocks of gulls flying in one direction over the city in the morning, and then in the opposite direction in the evening? Like your mom or dad might do, these gulls are commuting. After spending the night at a safe place like a reservoir, they're hungry. And where's the best place to find a meal in the city? The closest dump or transfer station is a good place to look.

Rock Pigeon

SCIENTIFIC NAME: *Columba livia*
LENGTH: 12½ in (32 cm)
WINGSPAN: 28 in (71 cm)

DURING THE 1600s, European immigrants brought the Rock Pigeon to America. Over the centuries, pigeons have spread throughout North and South America. Most pigeons live near people, especially in towns and cities, where they often nest on building ledges. The Rock Pigeon is a common sight in cities all around the world. Most pigeons are blue-gray with two dark wing bars. Many variations exist—from pure white to rusty brown to checkered— even in a single flock. The Rock Pigeon is also the ancestor of all domesticated pigeons. Many people around the globe keep pigeons as a hobby—breeding, training, and even racing them. In the same way that there are different dog breeds, there are hundreds of pigeon breeds.

VOICE

Courting birds make a series of throaty cooing sounds, *coo-cuk-cuk-cuk-cooo*. During courtship the male struts around the female while cooing, bowing, and inflating his throat. When taking flight, the pigeon's wings make a loud clapping sound.

FOOD

City birds will gather around anyone handing out bread-crumbs or other food tidbits, often eating right from the hand. In parks and on city streets they peck at the ground in search of seeds and other food. Baby pigeons are fed "pigeon's milk," a milky secretion from the bird's crop (part of its throat, also used for storing food).

HABITAT & RANGE

Rock Pigeons don't migrate; they live in the same place all year, even in the coldest areas. City streets and parks are often full of pigeons; in fact it's hard to avoid them in many cities. They also live in suburban and rural areas, especially around farm buildings. Pigeons found in city streets and parks are usually very tame.

PIGEONS **reuse** their nests many times, and the nests grow larger and sturdier over time.

A CLOSER LOOK

Pink legs and feet; when walking the head bobs back and forth.

Glossy neck and red eye

Variable plumage, but most pigeons have two dark wing bars and a white rump.

RANGE MAP KEY

YEAR-ROUND

WORLD WAR II HERO

The Dickin Medal, awarded to military animals for conspicuous gallantry during wartime, was given to G.I. Joe, a WW II carrier pigeon credited with preventing an Allied-occupied Italian village from being bombed. After receiving the medal in 1946, G.I. Joe served out his retirement at Fort Monmouth, New Jersey, and died in 1961 at the age of 18.

European Starling

EUROPEAN STARLINGS are tough birds to like. They are an invasive species, imported from Europe by immigrants. They're aggressive, pushing native birds like woodpeckers, bluebirds, and titmice out of their nest holes and taking them over. During nesting season they fight with each other over territory. They don't sing nicely, and there are millions of them. On the other hand, when the sun hits their plumage just right it glows with a glossy shine of green and purple, and it's a thrilling sight to see a winter flock take to the sky all at once. In early summer you are likely to see the black-feathered parents followed around by brownish juveniles begging for food, before they learn to find their own meals.

SCIENTIFIC NAME: *Sturnus vulgaris*
LENGTH: 8½ in (22 cm)
WINGSPAN: 16 in (41 cm)

VITAL STATISTICS

VOICE

The starling's song—if you can call it that—is an amazing mix of rattles, buzzes, clicks, and squealing notes, such as *zzzrt, pssst, pop, wheeeooo, shewheeeer*. They also copy (mimic) the songs of many other birds.

FOOD

Starlings are not picky eaters, which could be the reason there are so many of them. They eat almost anything and are especially fond of insects, spiders, and earth-worms, searching for them by digging around in the grass with their pointed bills. They also eat fruits, berries, and seeds.

HABITAT & RANGE

European Starlings prefer to live where people do. During the nesting season the male fights off other birds that want its nest site—usually an old woodpecker hole, a sheltered spot on the side of a building, or a birdhouse meant for another type of bird. In the city they nest in streetlights and traffic signals. In winter they're friendlier

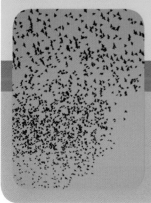

YOUNG starlings have brown feathers, but grow glossy adult **feathers** by the time they are **one** year old.

A CLOSER LOOK

Pointed yellow bill used for prying apart blades of grass in search of insects; bill turns black in winter.

Chunky body

Glossy green and purple plumage, otherwise looks black; in fall and winter its body is covered with white spots.

Short tail and pointed wings

Adult

and hang out in flocks with black-birds, grackles, and other starlings. Some winter flocks contain thou-sands of birds. Starlings live in every U.S. state and Canadian province.

RANGE MAP KEY

SUMMER (breeding)

YEAR-ROUND

SHAKESPEARE AND THE STARLING

It's because of the famous writer William Shakespeare that we are over-whelmed with starlings. In 1890, a group of people who loved Shakespeare's work thought it would be a great idea to bring to the United States every bird mentioned in his plays and poetry. Oops, bad idea. They released about 100 starlings in New York City's Central Park and the birds spread fast. By 1950 they could be found from coast to coast. Today about 200 million starlings live in North America.

House Sparrow

HOUSE SPARROWS originally came from Europe and Asia, but they didn't fly here on their own. As with European Starlings (see pp. 62–63), immigrants brought them here. One hundred House Sparrows were released in Brooklyn in 1851. By 1943 their population in North America was 150 million birds. How was that huge increase in numbers possible? First, House Sparrows like to live near people and can survive where most other birds can't. Second, they are very successful at raising families. A single pair usually nests three or four times every year and raises about 20 chicks. In five years a single pair could increase to 1,250 birds. Third, they are tough competitors that can take over nest sites from native birds.

SCIENTIFIC NAME: *Passer domesticus*
LENGTH: 6¼ in (16 cm)
WINGSPAN: 9½ in (24 cm)

VITAL STATISTICS

VOICE

The House Sparrow's most common call is a honest-to-goodness *chirp* or *cheep*. In winter, when birds flock together, their chattering can sound like a room full of talkative people.

FOOD

On city streets it's hard to tell what House Sparrows are finding to eat when they peck at the pavement, even if you watch closely. They are looking for tiny scraps of food that have collected in the cracks. In summer, House Sparrows also seek out grassy areas and shrubs to search for insects. Sometimes they even pick dead insects off car grills. In winter, they survive mostly on weed seeds and food scraps.

HABITAT & RANGE

House Sparrows are very common in most cities. Crevices and ledges on city buildings, suburban houses, and backyards offer places for nesting. In city parks they also nest in old woodpecker holes. The rough-and-tumble male House Sparrow often takes a nest hole away from a less aggressive bird, such as a chickadee, titmouse, or bluebird. House Sparrows were also introduced to South America, southern Africa, Australia, and New Zealand.

IN WINTER, House Sparrows form small flocks and **defend** a sheltered place to spend the night.

A CLOSER LOOK

Heavy bill for cracking seeds and catching large insects

Male's black throat and upper chest looks like a bib—the male with the biggest bib is at the top of the pecking order and the first to feed.

Male has black, reddish brown, and gray feathers; female looks brownish with darker streaks.

Fall male

Summer male

Chunky body and big head

Strong legs and feet used for hopping on the ground

RANGE MAP KEY

YEAR-ROUND

OPEN SESAME!

Turns out House Sparrows have some amazing ways of getting something to eat. Some birds in Australia figured out that a fast-food restaurant had doors that automatically opened when an "electric eye" was tripped. Male House Sparrows learned to flutter in front of it until the doors opened; then they flew in to pick dinner off the floor. Some females had a different tactic. They perched right on the electric eye and leaned over until the switch was tripped and the door opened. Not bad for a "bird brain."

Mini-Profiles

CITY STREETS AND PARKS

City parks are bird magnets. The park doesn't need to be big, and if it includes a grove of tall trees or a small pond, even better. See if you can spot some of the city and parks birds shown here.

MALLARD

SCIENTIFIC NAME: *Anas platyrhynchos*
LENGTH: 23 in (58 cm)
WINGSPAN: 35 in (89 cm)

The Mallard is the most abundant duck in the world and the ancestor of almost all domestic ducks. Just about every city park with a pond has a flock of half-tame Mallards in a zany mix of colors. Some are migratory wild birds, but others are year-round residents who vary from all-white to all-green to a patchwork of in-between colors. Most food is obtained by "tipping up"—using the familiar "butt-in-the-air-and-head-underwater" position that allows food to be picked off the pond bottom. City ducks are always on the lookout for a handout from visitors.

EURASIAN COLLARED-DOVE

SCIENTIFIC NAME: *Streptopelia decaocto*
LENGTH: 12½ in (32 cm)
WINGSPAN: 22 in (56 cm)

Eurasian Collared-Doves are the new guys on the block. Normally they live in Europe, Asia, and northern Africa. Their invasion of North America started in the Bahamas: After a few birds escaped from a pet shop during a burglary in 1974, the pet shop owner released about 50 more birds. From the Bahamas they made it to Florida by 1978. Since then, they have spread west to California and north to parts of southern Canada. Their colonization of North America is astonishing for its speed and success. They often are seen alongside our native Mourning Doves but are larger and paler.

CHIMNEY SWIFT

SCIENTIFIC NAME: *Chaetura pelagica*
LENGTH: 5¼ in (13 cm)
WINGSPAN: 14 in (36 cm)

The Chimney Swift looks like a "cigar with wings." Swifts spend the summer months flying over city and countryside searching for tiny flying insects. True to their name, they nest in chimneys and on the walls of abandoned buildings. Swifts build strange nests of twigs, glued together and attached with their sticky saliva to a wall inside the chimney. They gather in large flocks before migrating to South America for the winter.

MONK PARAKEET

SCIENTIFIC NAME: *Myiopsitta monachus*
LENGTH: 11½ in (29 cm)
WINGSPAN: 19 in (48 cm)

Yes, there really are parrots living in cities, and not only in "tropical" Miami or Los Angeles. Monk Parakeets are native to South America, but they are able to withstand the freezing temperatures of cities as far north as Chicago and New York. Many are pet birds that escaped their cages or were set free by their owners to form small colonies in the wild. They build large ball-like nests from thousands of sticks. A single nest can be home to a dozen or more families and is used throughout the year for shelter.

COMMON GRACKLE

SCIENTIFIC NAME: *Quiscalus quiscula*
LENGTH: 12½ in (23 cm)
WINGSPAN: 17 in (43 cm)

Up close, the Common Grackle's plumage shimmers with iridescent blue, purple, and bronze colors, set off by striking yellow eyes and a long, flared tail. From a distance, it just looks solid black. Most Common Grackles live east of the Rocky Mountains. In cities, grackles can be seen strutting across lawns and playing fields searching for insects and seeds or poking into open trash cans. The grackle's song is not a thing of beauty. Its throaty *readle-eek* and high-pitched whistles have been described as sounding like a rusty gate.

GREAT-TAILED GRACKLE

SCIENTIFIC NAME: *Quiscalus mexicanus*
LENGTH: 18 in (46 cm)
WINGSPAN: 23 in (58 cm)

The Great–tailed Grackle looks like a supersized Common Grackle. The male has glossy purple plumage and a huge tail; the female is brownish and about half as big as the male. Great-tailed Grackles live west of the Mississippi River, and they are found from Texas all the way to southern California. In cities, Great-tails often hang out together in parks and other places with large grassy lawns. They stay up late at night, and people who live near a roosting flock often complain about being kept awake by the birds' nonstop whistles, squeals, rattles, and other weird sounds.

BARN SWALLOW

Farms
and Fields

Farms and Fields

HABITAT

EASTERN BLUEBIRD

WILD TURKEY

LIVING THE COUNTRY LIFE

If you are visiting or live in a rural area east of the Rocky Mountains, you don't have to look very hard to see cows, sheep, and horses. But, try being a sharp-eyed bird-watcher and spot the many wild birds that share the land with us. With a little bit of luck and patience you'll find them. Explore the brushy edges of overgrown fields and any nearby woods—these places often have different species. The tall trees around a farmhouse are also good places to look for birds.

GREAT HORNED OWL

AMERICAN CROW

BARN SWALLOW

Wild Turkey

THE TURKEY we like to eat at Thanksgiving is a domesticated version of a wild bird still roaming the fields and forests of North America and Mexico. The Aztec were already raising turkeys for food when the Spanish conquistadores arrived, and domesticated turkeys were soon shipped back to Europe. Today, turkeys are farmed around the world. The unusual bare skin of the Wild Turkey's head is colored blue and red, and its chunky body is cloaked in coppery brown feathers. Small flocks walk on the ground searching for nuts, berries, and insects to eat, then fly up into a tree to spend the night in safety. Benjamin Franklin wanted the Wild Turkey to be the national bird of the U.S., but was outvoted by supporters of the Bald Eagle.

SCIENTIFIC NAME: *Meleagris gallopavo*
LENGTH: 46 in (117 cm)
WINGSPAN: 64 in (163 cm)

VITAL STATISTICS

VOICE

The gobble of a turkey is made only by males. It serves to attract females and drive off competing males. A gobbling male can be heard as far away as a mile (1.6 km) and if other males hear the gobbling they may respond, setting off a gobble extravaganza. How's that for talkin' turkey?

FOOD

Acorns, acorns, and more acorns. Grass seed, tree buds, crawling insects, grasshoppers, and ticks are also eaten with relish. Some turkeys live where oak trees and acorns aren't common and they do just fine on a diet of other tree nuts, plant seeds, insects, and the occasional leafy green.

HABITAT & RANGE

By the mid-1800s turkeys were rare birds in the United States. Too much hunting and cutting down of forests were the main reasons for their decline. Now they've been successfully reestablished over their former range and even beyond. Turkeys don't migrate; they live in the same area all year long. Since they travel almost completely on foot, they don't wander very far from where they were hatched.

BABY TURKEYS (called poults) can **feed themselves** as soon as they hatch.

A CLOSER LOOK

The female is smaller than the male and less iridescent.

Plumage is iridescent copper, blue, and green.

Naked blue and red head

Males have a "beard," a feathery tuft growing from his chest.

Turkeys are fast runners and have strong legs.

RANGE MAP KEY

 YEAR-ROUND

TOM "THE TERRIBLE" ATTACKS

Male Wild Turkeys in the U.S. are called toms, and sometimes they have temper tantrums and go a bit crazy. This is probably because they are protecting territories. Mail carriers have been chased down the street and even their mail trucks have been assaulted. Joggers have had to turn into sprinters to escape an angry "Tom." A television reporter in Sacramento, California, ended up chased down the street and trapped in her car, screaming, "Leave me alone!"

Great Horned Owl

THE GREAT HORNED is the biggest, baddest owl in North America. Its silhouette looks like a barrel-shaped body with "horns." You might see one at dusk or dawn, when it perches in the top of a tree. The "horns" are actually soft feathers that stick up from the top of its head. Some people think those are ears . . . wrong! An owl has large ear openings hidden under feathers on either side of its head. Like a spy plane, the Great Horned Owl flies on silent wings. It has huge eyes that can see in the dark, and its head is like a radar dish that can swivel 270 degrees. The owl has 3-D hearing that can locate prey hiding under leaves or snow, even when it's pitch-dark out. And not much escapes the clutches of its very sharp talons.

SCIENTIFIC NAME: *Bubo virginianus*
LENGTH: 22 in (56 cm)
WINGSPAN: 44 in (112 cm)

VOICE

Hoots are deep and mellow and often given in a set of five syllables: *hoo hoo-HOO hoooo hoo*. Listen for them calling from the time it gets dark until about midnight, and then again just before sunrise. If you do a good imitation of this owl's call, it might call back to you.

FOOD

The Great Horned Owl's favorite prey is mammals such as mice, rats, opossums, and rabbits, but sometimes they even eat skunks, porcupines, and armadillos! This owl has a very big mouth. Smaller prey get swallowed whole—head-first, bones and all. If the prey is too big to swallow in one gulp, the owl pulls it apart before eating it.

HABITAT & RANGE

In rural areas, the Great Horned Owl sometimes roosts in the hayloft of an abandoned barn, but it is usually seen perched in a tree. It can live anywhere from the Arctic Circle to the Sonoran Desert, in suburban neighborhoods, or deep in the forest. Only active at night, it spends the day roosting in a tree, unless discovered and mobbed by a gang of crows, its sworn enemies. The Great Horned Owl lives in the same area year-round.

GREAT HORNED OWLS weigh about three to four pounds (1.4 to 1.8 kg) but can **catch prey** up to about 10 pounds (4.5 kg)—the weight of a house cat!

A CLOSER LOOK

The "horns" are really just soft feathers. The large ears are located lower down.

Huge yellow eyes can spot prey from far away.

Wing feathers have soft edges so that a flying owl is completely silent.

Brown plumage with bars and speckles is good camouflage.

Very sharp talons are used for catching prey.

RANGE MAP KEY

YEAR-ROUND

DOWN THE HATCH ... AND UP AGAIN!

Owls swallow most of their prey whole—for Great Horned Owls that can be anything up to the size of a small rabbit. Later on, it spits up (regurgitates) a compact pellet of bones and fur, stuff it can't digest.

American Crow

THE AMERICAN CROW is a large black bird that everybody seems to recognize. Often, before you see a flock of crows, you can hear them cawing. If you listen very closely, you will notice different types of caws, depending on what they are communicating to other crows. They might be saying: "All clear, everything's okay" or "Come over here, I found something good to eat" or "DANGER! I see an owl." Crows are bold and intelligent, and when they see something new, they go to investigate. They live in close-knit family flocks. Some "teenaged" birds in the flock act as guards that watch for danger, or as scouts that search for food; others are "mother's helpers" who assist with feeding the nestlings.

SCIENTIFIC NAME: *Corvus brachyrhynchos*
LENGTH: 17½ in (45 cm)
WINGSPAN: 39 in (99 cm)

VOICE

American Crows usually make the harsh cawing sounds *caw, caw, caw, caw*. They also make a "rattle call" that sounds like a fingernail stroking the teeth of a comb and a variety of other calls that send specific messages to other members of their flock. In the East, there's another kind of crow, the Fish Crow. One way to tell them apart is by sound. The Fish Crow says *uh-uh uh-uh*.

FOOD

Crows eat an amazing variety of foods—whatever is easiest to get. During the warmer months, they eat insects and earthworms and sometimes prey on the eggs of other birds. Crows will eat mice, young turtles, and human garbage. They also chow down on crops of grains, seeds, nuts, and fruits, which is why farmers invented scarecrows. Winter flocks often rely on finding waste grain that was left in fields after the harvest.

HABITAT & RANGE

There are more than 30 different species of crows in the world. American Crows live all across the United States and in parts of Canada.

CROWS fly in straight lines. The phrase "as the crow flies" means going somewhere by the most **direct** route, just as a crow does.

A CLOSER LOOK

The heavy black bill is a useful tool for grabbing anything edible, from an earthworm on the ground to corn kernels on a corncob, or even for tearing open a garbage bag.

Glossy, black plumage, but it can look paler when the sun reflects off it

Males and females look identical, but young birds have brownish feathers that are not glossy.

Strong legs and feet for walking on the ground

Farmland and rural areas are especially attractive to crows—they prefer open areas with scattered trees. Winter flocks search out groves of trees where they spend the night together. Most crows that nest in Canada migrate to the United States in winter.

RANGE MAP KEY

- SUMMER (breeding)
- WINTER (nonbreeding)
- YEAR-ROUND

CROWS HATE OWLS

When a flock of crows discovers a sleeping Great Horned Owl (see pp. 74–75) they go crazy—making screeching caws, flying at the owl, and even pecking it. (This behavior is called mobbing.) If the owl flies off, the crows chase it for long distances. After dark, the tables are turned and the Great Horned Owl goes on the attack. Great Horned Owls kill and eat both adult crows and nestling crows, so it is understandable why crows and owls don't get along.

Barn Swallow

ONE OF THE MOST POPULAR birds of summer, the graceful Barn Swallow swoops over fields and pastures across North America and well beyond its borders. The Barn Swallow is the most widely distributed and abundant swallow in the world. A long, forked tail—it is North America's only swallow with a "swallowtail"— and slender body give it an elegant appearance. In flight, the tail can be spread (when banking or landing) or, more often, folded into a long point. Barn Swallows cruise for insects just a few inches above the ground or over water. Like other swallows, Barn Swallows are often seen perched on telephone wires.

SCIENTIFIC NAME: *Hirundo rustica*
LENGTH: 6¾ in (17 cm)
WINGSPAN: 15 in (38 cm)

VOICE

The Barn Swallow's song is a long series of scratchy, warbling phrases, interspersed with a grating rattle. Its flight call is a high-pitched *chee-jit*.

FOOD

Flying insects, including bees, wasps, flying ants, butterflies, and moths, are a Barn Swallow's food favorites.

HABITAT & RANGE

Barn Swallows have three basic habitat requirements: open areas for foraging (fields, pastures, golf courses, large yards); a man-made structure to shelter its nest (barn, culvert, bridge, pier, porch); and a body of water that provides mud for nest building. They avoid deserts and dense forest. Most Barn Swallows that nest in North America fly all the way to Central or South America for the winter. These birds live on all the world's continents, except chilly Antarctica where there are almost no flying insects to eat.

BARN SWALLOWS are very graceful fliers that can easily **swoop** through an open barn door to reach their nest and **feed their young.**

A CLOSER LOOK

Females have shorter tails than males, and young birds have very short tails.

Although its bill is small, the Barn Swallow has a wide mouth that helps it catch flying insects as large as moths and butterflies.

A long, forked tail helps the Barn Swallow make tight turns and dives.

Glossy, blue back and reddish brown throat

RANGE MAP KEY

SUMMER (breeding)	WINTER (nonbreeding)
MIGRATION	YEAR-ROUND

GIMME SHELTER

A nesting platform added to a porch or open garage is a good place for Barn Swallows to build their nest of mud and straw. Nowadays, they rarely nest anywhere other than in or on a man-made building. Before people built houses, barns, and bridges, Barn Swallows nested in caves.

Eastern Bluebird

EASTERN BLUEBIRDS have beautiful colors and millions of adoring fans. For hundreds of years, poems and songs like "The Bluebird of Happiness" have been written about them, and it's considered good luck to see one. In fact, they are the official state bird of both Missouri and New York. Fifty years ago, bluebirds were in trouble. Introduced species such as European Starlings and House Sparrows had taken over the nest holes that bluebirds needed to raise their families. But people came to the rescue and put up millions of nest boxes just for bluebirds, designed to keep those other birds out. Sometimes the bluebird houses are evenly spaced along a fence or country road that borders a field—this is called a "bluebird trail."

SCIENTIFIC NAME: *Sialia sialis*
LENGTH: 7 in (18 cm)
WINGSPAN: 13 in (33 cm)

VOICE

Eastern Bluebirds have a simple musical song that consists of a rich warble: *chur chur-lee chur-lee*. Males trying to attract a mate often sing from a high perch or even while in flight. After they start to nest, they are much quieter.

FOOD

From spring to early fall, bluebirds feast on insects. To hunt for an insect, a bluebird perches on a fence or low branch and stares at the ground looking for any movement. When it spies something it quickly flies down and grabs it in its bill. In winter, when insects are hard to find, bluebirds eat lots of berries and small fruits.

HABITAT & RANGE

If you live east of the Rocky Mountains in an area with open fields and trees, chances are you have Eastern Bluebirds as neighbors. They are usually easy to spot because they like to perch on fences and low branches, right out in the open. As you ride home from school, look for a flash of brilliant blue along the roadside—it's probably Mr. or Ms. Bluebird. Most of the bluebirds

TO SEE bluebirds up close, try feeding them mealworms. Put live **mealworms** in a shallow bowl outside in the morning and evening.

A CLOSER LOOK

The small, dark bill is good for catching insects but not strong enough to chisel a nest hole into a tree trunk. That's why bluebirds have to nest in an old woodpecker hole or a man-made birdhouse.

Large, dark eyes are good at spotting insects on the ground, even from far away.

The male has deep blue upper parts and a warm reddish brown breast; the colors are paler and grayer in the female. Juvenile bluebirds have spots.

Males

that nest in Canada and the Upper Midwest migrate to warmer southern areas for the winter.

RANGE MAP KEY

- SUMMER (breeding)
- WINTER (nonbreeding)
- YEAR-ROUND

LOOK AT ME

A male Eastern Bluebird works hard to find a mate. First he stakes a claim to a birdhouse or nest cavity and defends it from all others. Then, he brings nest material to the hole and constantly goes in and out. To make sure any nearby females see him, he flashes his blue wings, holding one wing high in the air and then the other. After mating, the female builds the nest and incubates the eggs.

Mini-Profiles

FARMS AND FIELDS

Some birds need more space than others. Farm fields and woodlots offer great places for birds to nest and find food. See if you can spot one of these birds when you're out in wide-open spaces.

RED-SHOULDERED HAWK

SCIENTIFIC NAME: *Buteo lineatus*
LENGTH: 17 in (43 cm)
WINGSPAN: 40 in (102 cm)

L arge and boldly colored, the Red-shouldered Hawk is common in rural and suburban parts of the eastern United States and also in California. Pretty, reddish brown feathers on its shoulders (where the wing bends) contrast with its tail of black and white bands. Listen in spring for a pair of courting Red-shoulders to loudly proclaim their territory—screaming *KEE-ahh* back and forth to each other—while circling high above the forest. They like to nest in woods near a stream or river where they can hunt for small mammals, frogs, snakes, and lizards.

EASTERN KINGBIRD

SCIENTIFIC NAME: *Tyrannus tyrannus*
LENGTH: 8½ in (23 cm)
WINGSPAN: 15 in (38 cm)

T he Eastern Kingbird is a close relative of the Western Kingbird (p. 148), but it lives across a much larger area of North America than its western cousin. In summer, the Eastern Kingbird nests from the East Coast across the northern prairies and all the way to Pacific coast of British Columbia, Canada. The two types of kingbirds also look different from each other: The Eastern is dressed in a snazzy outfit of dark gray and white, while the Western Kingbird has a yellow belly and a pale gray head. The Eastern Kingbird is also more of a world traveler. In fall, it migrates to the Amazon region of South America. The Western Kingbird is content to spend the winter in Mexico and Central America.

PURPLE MARTIN

SCIENTIFIC NAME: *Progne subis*
LENGTH: 8 in (20 cm)
WINGSPAN: 18 in (46 cm)

P urple Martins are insect-eating machines that catch their prey in flight—everything from dragonflies to tiny midges. These birds love the company of other martins. In the East they only nest in man-made martin houses—apartments that can hold 20 or more families—or hollow gourds hung in groups. They may squabble over the best locations, but they rarely nest alone. The males are deep purple-black and the females are similar but have pale bellies. In the fall, they form huge flocks that stay together until they reach their winter home in the Amazon.

TREE SWALLOW

SCIENTIFIC NAME: *Tachycineta bicolor*
LENGTH: 5¾ in (15 cm)
WINGSPAN: 14½ in (37 cm)

Tree Swallows are common around marshes and open fields. These steely blue and white birds are often seen flying over rivers, ponds, and fields as they chase down flying insects. Most Tree Swallows nest in old woodpecker holes or in birdhouses provided by people. In the winter months and during migration, Tree Swallows gather in marshy areas in flocks of thousands of birds, where they roost together during the night. When flying insects are unavailable, Tree Swallows can survive on a diet of berries. This ability allows them to linger in fall and to spend the winter farther north than any other swallow.

SONG SPARROW

SCIENTIFIC NAME: *Melospiza melodia*
LENGTH: 6 in (15 cm)
WINGSPAN: 8¼ in (21 cm)

If you see a small, brown bird with streaks poking around your backyard or along the brushy edges of a field, consider the Song Sparrow first—it's the most common sparrow in North America. Take a look at the streaks on the center of its breast, which usually come together to form a larger spot or "stickpin." In spring and summer, the male proclaims his territory from an eye-level perch by singing a loud and musical song that ends in a trill. Song Sparrows living in backyards and around farms often become quite tame, especially if you scatter birdseed on the ground for them.

INDIGO BUNTING

SCIENTIFIC NAME: *Passerina cyanea*
LENGTH: 5½ in (14 cm)
WINGSPAN: 8 in (20 cm)

In spring and summer, the male Indigo Bunting sings for hours on end from the top of a tree. The male is colored an intense blue that varies from sky blue to deep purple-blue on his head. The female is more reserved and stays hidden in nearby shrubs and high weeds where her nest is located. Her colors are brown and tan with just a hint of blue on her wings. This drab coloration helps to keep her hidden from predators. Indigo Buntings live in farm country throughout the American East and the Great Plains. In fall, birds migrate to Florida, the West Indies, Mexico, and Central America.

BROWN PELICAN

Beach
and Bay

Beach and Bay
HABITAT

BROWN PELICAN

SANDERLING

BIRDS LOVE THE SEASHORE

You'll always see a few gulls and sandpipers loafing on a sandy beach, but if you want to see birds in action—and lots of them—check out a nearby salt marsh or quiet bay. Birds are always on the lookout for a meal, and those are places where they can find lots to eat.

HERRING GULL

OSPREY

BLACK SKIMMER

Sanderling

SANDERLINGS SPEND MOST of the year at the beach, but they're not there to relax. Just the opposite—they're constantly in motion. Like little yo-yos with legs, they run ahead of incoming waves and seem to chase retreating ones. If you watch closely, you'll see that they are hunting for food in the wet sand. When a wave goes out they run forward onto the wet sand and pick through it for small crabs or tiny worms. But they have to be quick, because the next wave is on its way and Sanderlings don't like to go swimming. When not feeding, flocks roost together in sheltered dunes or along the high tide line amid seaweed and driftwood. Females lay eggs that are olive green to pale brown in color and spotted with black and brown.

SCIENTIFIC NAME: *Calidris alba*
LENGTH: 8 in (20 cm)
WINGSPAN: 17 in (43 cm)

VITAL STATISTICS

VOICE

Although the Sanderling doesn't have a real song, it does make a variety of calls and other sounds. Birds in winter flocks stay in touch with each other by twittering softly.

FOOD

Most of the year is spent on wave-swept sandy beaches where Sanderlings hunt for invertebrate animals in the wet sand—small crabs, marine worms, and horseshoe crab eggs are favorites. When nesting on the Arctic tundra during the summer, they switch to eating insects, which are plentiful there at that time of year.

HABITAT & RANGE

Hardly any people live where Sanderlings nest—the tundra of remote High Arctic areas. Summer in that part of the world is very short so they only stay for a couple of months. The rest of the year is spent on sandy beaches as far south as southern South America, southern Africa, Southeast Asia, and even Australia. Some individuals make a round-trip migration of over 12,000 miles (19,312 km). If you see a Sanderling at the beach in June,

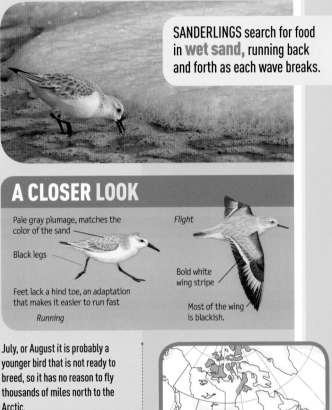

SANDERLINGS search for food in **wet sand,** running back and forth as each wave breaks.

A CLOSER LOOK

Pale gray plumage, matches the color of the sand

Black legs

Feet lack a hind toe, an adaptation that makes it easier to run fast

Running

Flight

Bold white wing stripe

Most of the wing is blackish.

July, or August it is probably a younger bird that is not ready to breed, so it has no reason to fly thousands of miles north to the Arctic.

RANGE MAP KEY

- SUMMER (breeding)
- WINTER (nonbreeding)
- MIGRATION

A SUITABLE SUIT OF FEATHERS

The ghostly gray Sanderling that chases waves at the beach looks very different from the same bird while it is breeding in the Arctic. Before migrating north in May, the Sanderling molts in a new coat of feathers. Its head turns rusty red, and its back is a colorful mix of rusty red, black, and white. It would look very conspicuous on a sandy beach, but at its nest on the tundra it fits right in. It's a good thing, because there aren't many places to hide on the treeless tundra and it needs to stay hidden from predators.

Herring Gull

HERRING GULLS are sturdy gray birds with pure white heads, yellow bills with a red spot at the tip, and pinkish legs. In winter, they can be found along all of North America's coastlines, and they are year-round residents from the mid-Atlantic north to Canada, and around the Great Lakes. In spring, many Herring Gulls migrate to northern Canada to nest. They can handle almost any kind of weather, and they can survive on almost any kind of food they can find or steal from others. Some birds live in wild places and might follow foraging whales or dolphins to feed on small fish that are driven to the surface. But Herring Gulls don't mind being around people, and some birds seem to spend their entire lives hanging out around beach resorts and marinas.

SCIENTIFIC NAME: *Larus argentatus*
LENGTH: 25 in (64 cm)
WINGSPAN: 58 in (147 cm)

VOICE

Herring Gulls have a variety of calls, from a quiet *mew* to a sharp *ha-ha-ha-ha!* and trumpeting *keeyow, kyow-kyow-kyow.* If you have spent time near the ocean, you have probably memorized not just the sound of the crashing waves, but also the insistent calling of the gulls.

FOOD

Herring Gulls are omnivores— they gobble down just about anything, from shellfish to small fish and squid to worms and bugs. These birds aren't squeamish about eating at a garbage dump or squabbling for french fries from beachgoers either. They also scavenge for dead fish and other animals. Herring Gulls will raid the nests of other birds and eat their eggs and chicks, and some male Herring Gulls will even eat the chicks of neighboring Herring Gulls.

HABITAT & RANGE

Herring Gulls can be found in lots of different places, such as beaches, lakes, rivers, and mudflats. They are almost always in a location that has water nearby. In winter, they tend to hang out in groups—large flocks are often seen around garbage dumps and landfills.

A YOUNG Herring Gull's plumage is all brown and **speckled.** It takes about 3 1/2 years before a young bird looks like an adult.

A CLOSER LOOK

Gulls can drink seawater because they have a gland behind the bill that extracts the salt and lets the super salty liquid drip from the nostril.

The heavy bill has a hooked tip that can deal with many types of food—dead or alive.

Long wings allow a gull to soar without much flapping.

Like all other gulls, Herring Gulls have webbed feet and are good swimmers.

Pink legs are the color of bubblegum.

Adult

In summer, they nest in colonies on islands, barrier beaches, and elevated marshy areas where they can keep an eye out for predators. Herring Gulls are more common on the East Coast than the West Coast.

RANGE MAP KEY

	SUMMER (breeding)		WINTER (nonbreeding)
	MIGRATION		YEAR-ROUND

CLAMMING IT UP

Ever tried to open a hard-shell clam? It isn't easy, even with a special tool. But that hasn't stopped Herring Gulls from eating these tasty morsels. Their solution: Grab the clam in your bill, fly high in the air, aim for some rocks (or a paved road), and let go. If the clam doesn't crack to smithereens on the first drop, keep on trying.

Black Skimmer

THE BLACK SKIMMER is an unusual waterbird—its knife-like red-and-black bill is much longer on the lower half than the upper, a feature that fits its feeding method. The skimmer flies just above the water's surface with its long wings flapping high above its body, and its lower bill slicing through the water. When its lower bill touches a small fish, the upper bill snaps down, trapping the fish, which it then swallows. Because it finds its prey by touch, some Black Skimmers hunt at night when fish often swim closer to the surface.

Skimmers are often seen in flocks, and they nest in colonies. Most types of North American birds have many close relatives, but the Black Skimmer has only two other relatives on the planet: one in Africa and another in India.

SCIENTIFIC NAME: *Rynchops niger*
LENGTH: 18 in (46 cm)
WINGSPAN: 44 in (112 cm)

VITAL STATISTICS

VOICE

The hollow, nasal laughing *k'wukk waak* sound made by the Black Skimmer might remind you of a low-pitched squeaker toy that your dog enjoys playing with, or a honking bicycle horn. A flock of skimmers calling to each other makes a chuckling chorus.

FOOD

Black Skimmers eat fish and sometimes travel as much as five miles (8 km) from their colony in search of good places to skim for them. Since they swallow their prey whole, they can manage fish only up to five inches (12.7 cm) long—herring, mullet, and pipefish are among their favorites. They also may eat a few small crabs and shrimp.

HABITAT & RANGE

Black Skimmers nest on sandy or shell beaches and skim for fish in quiet lagoons, harbors, and bays. They have also colonized the Salton Sea, a salty inland lake in the desert near Los Angeles, California. Much of their coastal habitat has had houses built along it, but artificial islands that have been built out of the sand and mud dredged out of harbors and marinas have become important nesting sites for skimmers. They are year-round residents in southern California, the Gulf Coast, and southern Atlantic beaches. Skimmers are also found in Central and South America.

WITH THIS VIEW of the Black Skimmer's bill, you can see how it earned **nicknames** like "Cut-Water," "Knifebill," and "Scissorbill."

A CLOSER LOOK

Long wings allow the skimmer to fly just inches above the water.

Black-and-white plumage is very striking.

Just the lower, longer part of the bill slices through the water.

The pupils of the skimmer's eyes can narrow down into vertical slits, which reduces the glare off the water, like a built-in pair of sunglasses.

The tip of its bright red bill is black. The black pigment in the bill makes it stronger and less likely to beak if the bill hits an underwater rock while skimming.

RANGE MAP KEY

- SUMMER (breeding)
- WINTER (nonbreeding)
- MIGRATION
- YEAR-ROUND

WHEN I GROW UP ...

Looking totally unlike its parent, a baby skimmer has a lot of growing to do. Its fluffy plumage looks just like the sand, so predators won't see it (camouflage), and its nest is just a shallow, hollowed-out area with nothing added to it. When it hatches, its bill is short and the upper and lower parts are equal in length. Within four weeks the lower part is already longer, but it take months to grow to full-size.

93

Brown Pelican

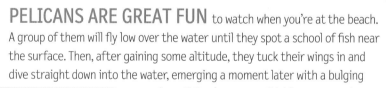

PELICANS ARE GREAT FUN to watch when you're at the beach. A group of them will fly low over the water until they spot a school of fish near the surface. Then, after gaining some altitude, they tuck their wings in and dive straight down into the water, emerging a moment later with a bulging pouch ... if they're successful. When not on the wing, they spend hours loafing on a dock, jetty, or sandy beach. The Brown Pelican was listed as an endangered species in 1970, its population depleted by hunting and pollution. But conservation measures, especially the banning of a pesticide called DDT, were so successful that the birds were taken off the list in 2009, and there are more pelicans now than there have ever been.

SCIENTIFIC NAME: *Pelecanus occidentalis*
LENGTH: 48 in (122 cm)
WINGSPAN: 84 in (213 cm)

VOICE

Pelicans rarely make any sounds except at the breeding colony. There the adults have low, hoarse calls. The nestlings keep up a steady squawking chorus, demanding to be fed.

FOOD

Fish, fish, and more fish, from tiny sardines to fish as large as mackerel. Sometimes when a pelican has a full pouch, a gull will reach in and steal a fish before the pelican can swallow it.

HABITAT & RANGE

The Brown Pelican is found close to warm seashore environments, but pelicans do visit southern California's salty Salton Sea located in the desert, more than 100 miles (161 km) from the ocean. They build their nests in short trees, shrubs, or on the ground. They tend to gather in colonies when nesting, often with other species such as gulls or herons. On the Atlantic coast, their nesting grounds are mainly on small islands covered with low-growing vegetation. The Channel Islands off southern California are home to many nesting pelicans because there are few people and lots of perfect spots to nest. In summer, some birds wander to the north.

DURING a dive, the pelican **folds** back its wings so they won't break, and it hits the water bill-first.

A CLOSER LOOK

The pouch is made of "rubbery" skin that can balloon out to hold more than three gallons (11.4 L) of water and fish.

Usually the pelican's neck is brown, but in winter it changes to white.

Its long toes are completely webbed, so swimming is a breeze. When landing on the water the pelican uses its huge feet as skids to help it stop.

Even the pelican's eyes can change color. Nobody is sure why, but they go from white to brown when nesting.

Pelicans are heavyweight birds, weighing about eight pounds (3.6 kg).

RANGE MAP KEY

SUMMER (breeding)

MIGRATION

YEAR-ROUND

A BILL AND A POUCH

A good fisherman needs good equipment, and Mother Nature has provided the pelican with some great gear—a really long bill with an amazing pouch of rubbery skin that can expand to hold gallons of water... and fish. As a pelican dives from the air into a school of fish, its pouch balloons open underwater, trapping both fish and water. Then the pelican comes to the surface, strains the water out of its pouch, and swallows the fish that are inside. Sashimi anyone?

Osprey

THE YELLOW-EYED OSPREY is the only North American hawk whose diet is almost 100 percent fresh fish. These birds have powerful wings that, over a 20-year life span, might carry the bird more than 160,000 miles (257,000 km) on migration. They build big nests of sticks high up on treetops, power poles, or in some cases on tall platforms provided by people. Generations of Ospreys will use the same nesting site, adding more sticks to it year after year. Once its nestlings have hatched, the Osprey carries its still squirming prey back to its nest, held firmly by sturdy claws. The Osprey's eggs don't all hatch at the same time. The first chick to hatch is the biggest and strongest, and often demands and gets more attention and food than the younger babies.

SCIENTIFIC NAME: *Pandion haliaetus*
LENGTH: 24 in (61 cm)
WINGSPAN: 63 in (160 cm)

VITAL STATISTICS

VOICE

The Osprey's voice is surprisingly high-pitched for such a large bird. Their call is a series of chirps that are spaced out: *eeee—eeee—eeee*. When they are alarmed, the chirps are closer together and rise in intensity; this may happen when an unfamiliar Osprey approaches the nest.

FOOD

Ospreys eat fish. Period. Over 80 species of fresh- and saltwater fish have been counted among their catches. The largest recorded fish caught was about 2¹/₂ pounds (1.1 kg), but most fish weigh between ¹/₃ and ²/₃ pound (150 to 300 g). When it is carrying a fish in its feet, the Osprey lines the fish up headfirst in the wind to reduce drag—it looks like the Osprey is toting a torpedo.

HABITAT & RANGE

Ospreys live around rivers, small and medium-size lakes, reservoirs, lagoons, bays, and salt marshes. Look for them flying over the water, or perched in a tall tree or on top of a power or

OSPREYS' stick nests are big enough for a **person** to sit in.

A CLOSER LOOK

Yellow eyes can correct for the distortion of the water and guide an Osprey directly to a fish. Young Ospreys have orange eyes.

Bold, dark eye stripes probably reduce glare off the water so Ospreys can better see beneath the surface.

Huge talons—four on each foot—and feet with rough, spiny bottoms make it impossible for a fish to escape once caught.

Strong wings measure about five feet (1.5 m) from tip to tip.

telephone pole or cell phone tower. Most Ospreys leave North America by late fall. Many migrate as far south as South America.

RANGE MAP KEY

- SUMMER (breeding)
- WINTER (nonbreeding)
- MIGRATION
- YEAR-ROUND

HIGH-DIVING CHAMP

Drawing a bead on a fish near the surface, this Osprey is unlikely to miss. With the style and accuracy of an Olympic diver, this big hawk isn't afraid to get a little wet—its dives can take it completely underwater. Its wings are folded back so that its bones don't break when it hits the water.

Beaches and coastal marshes are food factories for birds that eat fish and marine invertebrates like crabs, shellfish, and worms. Next time you're by the beach or bay, look for these birds.

SURF SCOTER

SCIENTIFIC NAME: *Melanitta perspicillata*
LENGTH: 20 in (51 cm)
WINGSPAN: 30 in (76 cm)

The male Surf Scoter is a black-and-white sea duck with a colorful bill; the female is dark brown with white patches on her head. Scoters spend the winter up and down the Pacific and Atlantic coasts, in bays and estuaries. They feed on mollusks (clams and mussels) and crustaceans (mostly crabs). Some immature scoters remain at the seashore all summer while the adults fly to freshwater lakes in the Arctic tundra to nest. Sometimes, the tundra lakes get so crowded that mother scoters lose track of their own chicks and feed someone else's babies. No one seems to mind.

AMERICAN OYSTERCATCHER

SCIENTIFIC NAME: *Haematopus palliatus*
LENGTH: 18½ in (47 cm)
WINGSPAN: 34 in (86 cm)

It's impossible not to notice the eye-catching American Oystercatcher with its large lipstick-red bill. These big shorebirds of the Atlantic and Gulf coasts often gather in small flocks at the best feeding locations: salt marshes, mudflats, and shellfish beds exposed at low tide. It uses its long, stout bill to probe for food and pry it open. Mussels, clams, oysters, crabs, and marine worms are all on the menu. On the Pacific coast, you may see the American Oystercatcher's close cousin, the Black Oystercatcher. Its plumage is completely black and it prefers rocky coastlines, but it has the same bright red bill.

RUDDY TURNSTONE

SCIENTIFIC NAME: *Arenaria interpres*
LENGTH: 9½ in (24 cm)
WINGSPAN: 21 in (53 cm)

Turnstones are short-legged, chunky-looking shorebirds named for their habit of flipping over stones, shells, and bits of seaweed with their pointed bills while searching for food. Social birds, they gather together in small flocks, chattering as they feed along rocky shores and pebbly beaches. Bold markings on the turnstone's wings, back, and tail are hard to miss when it flies. Like many shorebirds, turnstones nest in the Arctic, but spend most of the year on the seacoast and even around the Great Lakes.

WILLET

SCIENTIFIC NAME: *Tringa semipalmata*
LENGTH: 15 in (38 cm)
WINGSPAN: 26 in (66 cm)

The Willet looks drab standing on a beach or mudflat since its plumage is various shades of gray and brown. But when the Willet takes flight and flashes its bold black-and-white wing pattern, its identity becomes obvious. Willets breed in two very different habitats—prairie wetlands and eastern salt marshes. The ones breeding in salt marshes are smaller, darker, and have higher-pitched voices. Some scientists think that the two populations are so different that they are different species. The Willets that spend the winter on North American beaches are the larger, paler western birds.

CASPIAN TERN

SCIENTIFIC NAME: *Hydroprogne caspia*
LENGTH: 21 in (53 cm)
WINGSPAN: 50 in (127 cm)

The Caspian Tern is the biggest tern in the world—as big as a gull—with a thick red bill and black wing tips. Like many other terns, the Caspian cruises high over the water searching for something to eat. When a fish is spotted, the Caspian dives in headfirst to grab dinner in its bill. Coastal salt marshes, barrier islands, and islands in rivers and lakes are prime locations for a breeding colony. Nesting terns are very aggressive about defending their eggs and young from predators and people, so stay clear or risk getting dive-bombed. Young terns—even when fully grown—follow their parents around for months loudly begging for a free meal.

COMMON LOON

SCIENTIFIC NAME: *Gavia immer*
LENGTH: 32 in (81 cm)
WINGSPAN: 46 in (117 cm)

Loons are known for their weird yodeling call, which some people think is creepy when they first hear it. Most of their yodeling is done in summer on lakes in the northern U.S. and Canada where they nest. The rest of the year is usually spent in coastal areas, around bays and harbors. The Common Loon has huge webbed feet that propel it during dives in pursuit of the fish it feeds on. When a fish is caught, it's often swallowed underwater. You may see a loon swimming along with just its head underwater—"snorkeling"—while it's looking for a fish to chase after.

CALIFORNIA CONDOR

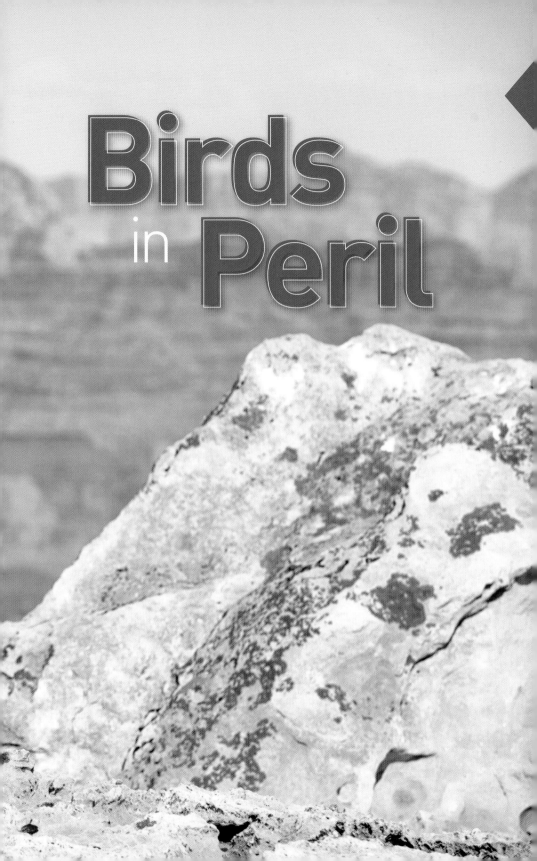

Birds
in Peril

BIRDS IN PERIL IN NORTH AMERICA

These birds are officially classified as "endangered" in North America. They have very small populations and need our protection to survive.

WHOOPING CRANE

SCIENTIFIC NAME: *Grus americana*
LENGTH: 52 in (132 cm)
WINGSPAN: 87 in (221 cm)

Because of habitat loss, the Whooping Crane—the tallest bird in North America—almost went extinct in the 1940s, when only 16 birds were left alive. Thanks to the efforts of conservationists in the U.S. and Canada, there are about 600 Whooping Cranes alive today. However, it remains an endangered species, breeding in northern Canada and wintering on the Texas Gulf Coast. One captive breeding program teaches young birds their migration route by leading them with ultra-light aircraft.

CALIFORNIA CONDOR

SCIENTIFIC NAME: *Gymnogyps californianus*
LENGTH: 47 in (119 cm)
WINGSPAN: 108 in (274 cm)

This huge, carrion-eating vulture is the largest flying bird in North America. Condors have a wingspan of up to nine feet (2.7 m) and can weigh over 25 pounds (11.4 kg). Once common from the Baja peninsula in Mexico to the Canadian border, the condor came close to the point of extinction in the 1980s. In 1987, the last nine birds—all living in the mountains of southern California—were caught and put into a captive breeding program. That program is a big success. Young captive-bred California Condors have been released into wilderness areas in California, Arizona's Grand Canyon, and the mountains of Baja California, Mexico. The first successful nesting in the wild was in 2003. By December 2015, 167 condors were living in captivity and 268 were flying free.

RED-COCKADED WOODPECKER

SCIENTIFIC NAME: *Picoides borealis*
LENGTH: 8½ in (22 cm)
WINGSPAN: 14 in (36 cm)

Twenty-two species of woodpeckers breed in North America, but only one, the Red-cockaded, is rare and endangered. It lives in old growth pine forests in the South. These black-and-white woodpeckers chisel out a nest cavity in a living pine tree. Due to the cutting of trees, there are not many forests left with the right kind of pine trees for these woodpeckers. Most Red-cockadeds are found in national forests and other conservation areas.

THICK-BILLED PARROT

SCIENTIFIC NAME: *Rhynchopsitta pachyrhyncha*
LENGTH: 16¼ in (41 cm)
WINGSPAN: 33 in (83 cm)

Thick-billed Parrots now live only in pine forests in the mountains of western Mexico and they are endangered there too. Until the 1950s they also lived in the mountains of Arizona and New Mexico near the Mexican border. Unfortunately, these beautiful green parrots with red crowns were hunted and trapped for the pet trade. Logging removed most of the old-growth pine forests that they need to survive. They nest in holes in the trunks of large trees and eat mainly pine seeds.

BLACK-CAPPED VIREO

SCIENTIFIC NAME: *Vireo atricapilla*
LENGTH: 4½ in (11 cm)
WINGSPAN: 7 in (18 cm)

In the U.S., the tiny Black-capped Vireo nests only in central Texas and a small part of Oklahoma—some of the hottest areas of North America. It has red eyes, a black cap, yellow-green upperparts, and two wing bars. In fall, all these vireos leave the U.S. and migrate to western Mexico for the winter. Habitat changes and parasitism by Brown-headed Cowbirds (p. 195) continue to threaten the small U.S. population of about 10,000 birds. Conservation efforts include the removal of cowbirds and keeping the Black-capped Vireos' breeding areas wild and undeveloped.

KIRTLAND'S WARBLER

SCIENTIFIC NAME: *Setophaga kirtlandii*
LENGTH: 5¾ in (15 cm)
WINGSPAN: 9 in (23 cm)

In the early 1970s fewer than 200 pairs of Kirtland's Warbler were alive in the world. This small warbler breeds only in stands of young jack pine trees in the state of Michigan. When the pines grow too big, the warblers have to move. New stands of young pines are created only by wildfires. Conservation efforts include two jobs: Eradicate as many parasitic cowbirds as possible where the warblers nest, and set controlled wildfires to make sure there are always enough young jack pines. These efforts are working. Today more than 1,800 pairs are alive.

Mini-Profiles

BIRDS IN PERIL AROUND THE WORLD

These are some of the most endangered bird species on Earth. International conservation organizations are working to save them from extinction. Since these birds are rare, it is not possible to verify their wingspans. Instead, we have provided weight for each species.

HOODED GREBE

SCIENTIFIC NAME: *Podiceps gallardoi*
LENGTH: 12½ in (32 cm)
WEIGHT: 1.4 lb (0.6 kg)

The Hooded Grebe is a beautiful waterbird discovered just 40 years ago. It nests on a few remote lakes in very desolate and wild parts of Patagonia, near the southern tip of South America. The entire world population is estimated to be only 800 birds. The number of birds has decreased at an alarming rate over the last 20 years, and they are critically endangered. Climate change is likely responsible for some of their breeding lakes drying up, and the careless introduction of non-native American minks that kill adults and chicks is also a serious threat.

GIANT IBIS

SCIENTIFIC NAME: *Thaumatibis gigantia*
LENGTH: 41 in (104 cm)
WEIGHT: 9.3 lb (4.2 kg)

There are fewer than 300 Giant Ibises alive today. Birds of this species are huge, dark ibises—the largest ibises in the world—with a featherless grayish head. Small groups search freshwater pools for food with their long downward curved bills, but almost nothing is known about what exactly they eat. Most of these birds live in northern Cambodia and a few in nearby Vietnam. Hunting is a continual threat, and its swampy habitat is threatened by logging and conversion to farmland. Climate change has led to the drying up of some swamps where the Giant Ibis lives. Because it is so rare and unusual, bird-watchers make special trips to look for it. The local community benefits from this tourism, which will hopefully lead to additional protection.

KAGU

SCIENTIFIC NAME: *Rhynochetos jubatus*
LENGTH: 21½ in (55 cm)
WEIGHT: 2 lb (0.9 kg)

This ghostly gray Kagu lives only in forests on the island of New Caledonia in the South Pacific. It is flightless and so unique that it is placed in its own family. Small groups of Kagus search the forest floor for earthworms, insects, snails, and lizards. No one knows exactly how many Kagus are left— maybe 1,000. Hunting dogs are the main threat to this flightless bird. Fortunately, hunting with dogs is decreasing. Education programs to promote pride in the Kagu are also helping. In some areas Kagus are increasing, but with so few birds on only one island, the species remains highly endangered.

SPOON-BILLED SANDPIPER

SCIENTIFIC NAME: *Calidris pygmaea*
LENGTH: 6¼ in (16 cm)
WEIGHT: 1 oz (30 g)

This tiny sandpiper uses the spoon-shaped tip of its bill to gather small insects and insect larvae found in shallow water and on mudflats. Unlike other endangered birds in this section, the Spoon-billed Sandpiper migrates great distances. It nests on the tundra in remote areas of the Russian Far East and spends the winter in a few coastal areas of Southeast Asia. Fewer than 400 birds exist, and their numbers are dropping. The threats are many: loss of tidal flats along its migration route and where it spends winters, pollution, hunting, and the effects of climate change.

PHILIPPINE EAGLE

SCIENTIFIC NAME: *Pithecophaga jefferyi*
LENGTH: 38 in (97 cm)
WEIGHT: 14 lb (6.5 kg)

The massive Philippine Eagle is the second largest eagle in the world and the most endangered. Fewer than 200 birds live in forested mountains, mostly on the Philippine island of Mindanao. They hunt for large tree-dwelling mammals, such as lemurs and monkeys. Large-scale logging operations and the clearing of forests for agriculture have severely reduced their habitat, and shooting and trapping is still common. Public education and protecting the few remaining forest areas where Philippine Eagles live can help, but it might be too late for this majestic bird.

KAKAPO

SCIENTIFIC NAME: *Strigops habroptila*
LENGTH: 25 in (64 cm)
WEIGHT: 5½ lb (2.5 kg)

The Kakapo is the most unusual parrot in the world. It has lost the ability to fly and is the heaviest parrot alive. This parrot is also nocturnal (active at night) and shuffles around on the dark forest floor hunting for seeds, berries, and fallen fruit. It originally lived on the North, South, and Stewart Islands of New Zealand, but it was killed for human food and then became prey for non-native predators. In an effort to save the species from extinction, all 61 remaining birds were moved to three tiny offshore islands with no non-native predators. All Kakapos are radio-tagged and tracked throughout the year. By 2016 the total population had increased to 157 birds.

6 Things You Can Do to Help Birds

1. KEEP CATS INDOORS

Every year, cats kill millions of wild birds. Pet cats do not have to go outside to hunt in order to have a good life. Some people think that putting a small bell around a cat's neck will warn birds and protect them, but this does not work.

2. PREVENT PICTURE-WINDOW COLLISIONS

Windows are among the major killers of wild birds. Sometimes, a big pane of glass can reflect the outdoors like a mirror. Birds can't tell that the glass is there and they fly right into it. Some birds are killed instantly by the impact. Others are merely stunned and will be able to fly away after a brief recovery, though some of those will die later from their injuries. If you have a big window or glass door that birds have crashed into, break up the reflections by covering the outside with decals, or hang suncatchers, crystals, or feathers, which work best if they sway in the wind. These must be close together over the entire surface of the glass in order to work.

3. FEED BIRDS IN YOUR YARD OR ON YOUR BALCONY

In parts of the country where winters are cold, birds sometimes struggle to find enough food when the temperature drops or snow covers the ground. Putting up bird feeders, or even scattering birdseed on the ground, greatly helps the birds that are living near you year-round. If you can, put up a suet feeder, available in many pet supply stores. Or make a peanut butter pinecone: Spread natural peanut butter on a pinecone and then roll it in unsalted sunflower seeds or peanuts. Try to hang it up where the squirrels can't get to it! Keep feeders clean.

foggers in your yard, and switch to natural, nontoxic methods of pest control for garden plants and flowers. Support farmers who are committed to growing food without using toxic chemicals by eating sustainably grown food as much as you can.

4. SAFELY DISCARD PLASTIC BAGS AND SIX-PACK HOLDERS

Birds who scavenge in landfills and dumps—especially gulls—can be injured or killed by getting their heads caught in the plastic loops that hold soda cans together. Before you throw them away or recycle them, take a pair of scissors and snip open every loop. Tie knots in plastic bags before you discard them, so that birds don't get trapped in them.

5. AVOID CHEMICAL PESTICIDES AS MUCH AS POSSIBLE

Insects are essential to the survival of many species of birds. Don't use chemical insect

6. BECOME A "CITIZEN SCIENTIST" IN YOUR OWN HOME

Project Feeder Watch, sponsored by Cornell University, is a great way to help birds, and everyone is welcome to participate. You identify and count birds coming to your feeder and transmit your data online—it becomes part of a huge database that helps scientists and conservationists who work to protect birds. For more information, check out the Project Feeder Watch website: *feederwatch.org*.

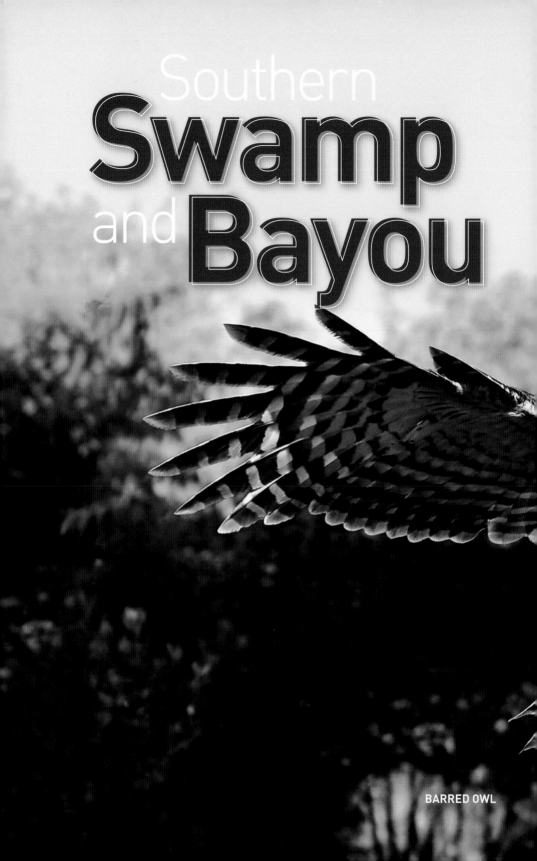

Southern
Swamp
and Bayou

BARRED OWL

Southern Swamp and Bayou

HABITAT

SNOWY EGRET

A UNIQUE PLACE TO LIVE

A swamp is a low-lying wooded area that is usually flooded with overflow from a nearby river or lake, and is full of plant and animal life. Tupelo, cypress, and other types of trees and vegetation get lots of water and grow lush. Bayous, found along the Gulf Coast, can be a slow-moving river or stream, or a marshy lake or wetland. Many types of animals—crayfish, shrimp, catfish, alligators, frogs, and a great variety of insects—are abundant in swamps and bayous, and so are the birds that feed on them.

BARRED OWL

ANHINGA

WOOD DUCK

LIMPKIN

Wood Duck

ALTHOUGH the Wood Duck looks as if could be a brightly painted wooden duck, it is named for its habitat choice—heavily wooded swamps and streams. They are one of the few ducks that can perch in trees, and they also nest in tree cavities. Male Wood Ducks have breathtaking colors in complicated patterns, and both males and females have bushy crests that make their heads look large and rounded. During the late 19th century, when Wood Duck populations were declining rapidly due to habitat loss and commercial hunting, some ornithologists worried that the Wood Duck would become extinct. But remote southern swamps offered the Wood Duck a safe haven. A federal ban on the hunting of Wood Ducks was enacted in 1918 and lasted until 1941 and, over time, the population recovered.

SCIENTIFIC NAME: *Aix sponsa*
LENGTH: 18 1/2 in (47 cm)
WINGSPAN: 30 in (76 cm)

VOICE

Female Wood Ducks make a high-pitched *ooo-eeek ooo-eeek!* when disturbed or taking flight. Males have a thin, rising and falling whistle, *zeeet!*

FOOD

Wood Ducks are able to forage in water, on land, and in trees. They eat water plants and grasses; tree seeds and acorns; wild berries, grapes, and cherries; and wheat, corn, and rice left in harvested fields. In summer, ducklings eat lots of insects and tiny animals, such as snails, because they need high-protein foods to grow.

HABITAT & RANGE

Wood Ducks do well in many watery places. Swamps and marshes work best for them, but wooded creeks, streams, and small rivers are also important breeding areas. Beaver ponds, with lots of vegetation and nearby trees, are ideal. They prefer to nest in natural tree cavities but sometimes use an old squirrel or Pileated Woodpecker nest hole. Nest boxes put up by people are also very popular.

WOOD DUCK ducklings are unable to fly until about two months old, but they **feed** themselves from the very start.

A CLOSER LOOK

In good light, the male's dark colors light up with blue, green, and bronze highlights.

Male

Unlike most ducks, Wood Ducks have strong claws for perching on branches.

The female has browner colors—better for camouflage—and a teardrop-shaped eye patch.

Female

Wood Ducks that breed in the north migrate south for the winter. Their only close relative, the Mandarin Duck, lives in Japan and China.

RANGE MAP KEY

- SUMMER (breeding)
- WINTER (nonbreeding)
- YEAR-ROUND

BABIES THAT BOUNCE

The day that a baby Wood Duck hatches, it faces a huge challenge. It's in a nest hole perhaps 50 or more feet (15.2 m) off the ground, and Mom is on the ground calling to her family to join her. Problem is, ducklings can't fly, so the only way down is to jump. Fortunately, ducklings are lightweight balls of fluff that usually just bounce off the ground unhurt. Once the whole family has made it, they stick close to Mom and she leads them to water.

Anhinga

THE ANHINGA is a large diving bird with a long neck, often seen along the edges of slow-moving streams and bayous in the American South and along the Gulf Coast. It can swim underwater with only its head and long, snake-like neck showing above the surface. The Anhinga's heavy bones and nonwaterproof feathers allow it to swim underwater with ease as it stalks fish. But wet feathers can't keep the Anhinga warm, so it spends long periods of time perched on a log with outstretched wings trying to dry off. The Anhinga is also a graceful flier and can stay aloft for long periods of time soaring on the air currents.

SCIENTIFIC NAME: *Anhinga anhinga*
LENGTH: 35 in (89 cm)
WINGSPAN: 45 in (114 cm)

VOICE

Usually silent, except during breeding season. Around their nest site, Anhingas make harsh and grating noises that sound like radio static.

FOOD

The Anhinga's favorite food is medium-size fish, including bass, mullet, pickerel, sunfish, sucker, and gizzard shad. If there aren't enough fish, the Anhinga will eat insects, crayfish, shrimp, and even snakes, baby alligators, frogs, and small turtles.

HABITAT & RANGE

Anhingas are aquatic birds, usually found in or near shallow, freshwater streams, cypress swamps, ponds, and marshy areas. They prefer locations with overhanging trees or fallen logs, where they can sit in the sun to warm up and dry their wings. Anhingas sometimes forage in brackish lagoons or tidal streams. They breed in colonies with other waterbirds, such as herons, egrets, ibises, storks, and

BABY ANHINGAS have downy white feathers and cannot fly until they are about two months old.

A CLOSER LOOK

During courtship, the male Anhinga's face turns brilliant green and blue.

Male's plumage is black with silvery spots and streaks; the female has a light brown neck and breast.

Female

The long, sharp bill is used to spear fish.

Huge webbed feet propel the Anhinga underwater.

The long tail has curious ridges running across it.

cormorants. Most Anhingas don't migrate, but live in the same place year-round. They also live in Mexico and in Central and South America.

RANGE MAP KEY

SUMMER (breeding)

MIGRATION

YEAR-ROUND

THE FISH DON'T STAND A CHANCE

Cruising underwater, the Anhinga searches for fish in shallow, weedy areas. Its neck bones have a special built-in hinge and muscles that allows it to thrust its daggerlike bill forward—like a lightning-fast speargun. Fish are usually impaled through the side with a partially open bill, which has backward-facing barbs so that the fish won't slip off. To eat, the fish is taken to the surface, flipped in the air, caught headfirst, and swallowed whole.

Snowy Egret

SNOWY EGRETS, WITH THEIR ELEGANT look, brilliant white plumage, and long, graceful legs are common in many wetland areas, but they were almost wiped out during the late 19th century. They were hunted for their beautiful white feathers, which were used to decorate women's hats. The Snowy Egret was saved by the efforts of early conservationists who started the Audubon Society in order to stop the killing of birds for the millinery (hat-making) trade. There are other species of all-white egrets, but you can identify a Snowy by its medium size, thin black bill, black legs, and yellow feet. Snowy Egrets may have small eyes, but their eyesight is excellent and helps them spot food.

SCIENTIFIC NAME: *Egretta thula*
LENGTH: 24 in (61 cm)
WINGSPAN: 41 in (104 cm)

VITAL STATISTICS

VOICE

Snowy Egrets are usually silent. When disturbed or agitated they make a variety of harsh croaks and other sounds, like someone clearing their throat or gargling.

FOOD

These birds are active—sometimes frantic—foragers in shallow water. They search for fish, insects, frogs, snakes, and lizards. They also eat aquatic invertebrates (animals without backbones living in water) like shrimp, crayfish, and crabs. Some of their food lives in freshwater, some in salt water, and some in brackish swamps, but to Snowy Egrets, they're all good.

HABITAT & RANGE

Snowy Egrets are found in many kinds of watery places—fresh- and saltwater marshes, sheltered bays and lagoons, ponds and bayous. They like to raise their families in groups (colonies), often building their nests of sticks in trees or shrubs near the water, or sometimes on the ground in marshy areas. In winter, northern birds leave areas where marshes and ponds freeze over. Snowy Egrets also live in Central and South America.

WHEN courting, long **curling** plumes grow from a Snowy Egret's back, the skin on its face turns red, and its feet turn orange.

A CLOSER LOOK

Long black legs allow the Snowy to wade out to where its favorite food lives.

Yellow feet attract the small minnows that the Snowy eats.

Black bill with a fine tip for grabbing minnows and small crustaceans, such as crayfish and shrimp

Long neck, usually held in an S-curve, can uncoil in a flash when the Snowy strikes at a fish.

RANGE MAP KEY

SUMMER (breeding)

WINTER (nonbreeding)

MIGRATION

YEAR-ROUND

MAGICAL GOLDEN SLIPPERS

This egret's yellow feet ("golden slippers") are more than just an easy way for people to identify it. Small fish and minnows—the Snowy's favorite food—are actually attracted to their color and movement. When a minnow comes by to investigate, it's like having takeout dinner delivered to the door. The Snowy also uses those magic feet to stir up the mud and scare hidden prey into view.

117

Limpkin

THE LIMPKIN is so unusual that it is placed in its own family, and it has no close relatives. Looking a bit like a cross between a heron and a rail (a secretive group of marsh birds), its evolution is a bit of a mystery. The Limpkin's plumage is brown with small white spots and streaks that help it remain hidden even though it is a big bird with a long neck. It is uncommon—you have to be in the right place to see one. In the U.S. it lives only in Florida swamps and wetlands where its favorite food, the apple snail, also lives. The weird screams, moans, and rattles of unseen males add further intrigue to an already mysterious bird. When it flies a specially shaped, outer wing feather vibrates to make a buzzing sound.

SCIENTIFIC NAME: *Aramus guarauna*
LENGTH: 26 in (66 cm)
WINGSPAN: 40 in (102 cm)

VOICE

Male Limpkins have elongated and looped windpipes that make their voices very loud. It is similar to the way the brass loops in a trumpet or tuba make those instruments loud. Both the male and the female make angry rattles and clucks when they sense danger, perhaps from a nearby alligator.

FOOD

The Limpkin eats apple snails and more apple snails. In the U.S. these big snails—the largest in the U.S.—are found only in marshes and swamps in Florida and southern Georgia. Using its bill like a tool, it takes the Limpkin only 10 to 20 seconds to pull a snail from its shell. In favorite feeding spots, piles of empty snail shells build up—the remains of many meals.

HABITAT & RANGE

In the U.S., the Limpkin lives only in Florida swamps, marshes, and along slow-moving rivers; it does not migrate. Corkscrew Swamp, Wakulla Springs, the Kissimmee River, and Lake Okeechobee are some places

IN FLIGHT the **Limpkin** stretches out its neck, unlike herons and egrets that fly with their necks pulled in.

A CLOSER LOOK

Dark brown upper-parts with white spots

Long dark legs help with wading. It does not limp as its name seems to imply, and is a good swimmer.

Long, slightly decurved bill—the perfect size and shape for hunting large snails and pulling them from their shells

Striped neck

to spot it. In the Corkscrew Swamp Sanctuary near Naples, Florida, a boardwalk winds through the swamp for over two miles (3.2 km). From this path, you can see all the bird species in this section as well as many others.

RANGE MAP KEY

▮ YEAR-ROUND

LET THEM EAT SNAILS

Have you ever eaten snails? In France they are called escargot (pronounced ess-car-go) and are very popular cooked with lots of garlic butter. Without the garlic butter, though, they might remind you of hot pencil erasers. The Limpkin eats raw snails and almost nothing else. The large apple snail is the perfect food for a Limpkin. The slight bend at the tip of the Limpkin's bill has just the right curve to pull the snail out of its shell. Then down the hatch.

Barred Owl

THE RICH MELLOW hooting call of the Barred Owl is commonly heard in southern swampland. This large owl is found in dense woodland all over the eastern half of the U.S. and in the Pacific Northwest. Almost as big as a Great Horned Owl (see pp. 74–75), the Barred Owl has a round head and no ear tufts. Though it is well camouflaged, the Barred Owl tends to fly away when its roost is approached, unless it lives in an area where people frequently pass by—for example, near a boardwalk in a swamp. In those situations, people are not perceived as a threat, and the owl will stay put and be easy to get a good look at. The Barred Owl is aggressive in defending its territory, but not as aggressive as the Great Horned Owl.

SCIENTIFIC NAME: *Strix varia*
LENGTH: 21 in (53 cm)
WINGSPAN: 42 in (107 cm)

VOICE

The Barred Owl is more often heard than seen. Its unique call is heard during the day more than any other owl's, and is easy to recognize: "who-cooks-for-you, who-cooks-for-YOU-ALL." The Barred Owl is often called "the eight-hooter," with its last hoot trailing downward. If you imitate its call, it may answer you.

BARRED OWLS sometimes **hunt** during the day, especially if the weather is cloudy or snowy.

FOOD

Because they have excellent hearing and night vision, Barred Owls are able to hunt at night. They catch and eat small mammals like mice, squirrels, and rabbits, but they also eat birds, snakes, lizards, frogs, fish, and large insects. In southern swamps, the Barred Owl's belly feathers can turn pink from eating lots of crayfish.

A CLOSER LOOK

Hooked, yellow bill (the large mouth that can swallow a whole mouse is hidden by feathers)

Huge, dark brown eyes that see well at night

Mostly brown plumage is spotted with white above and pale buff below with dark, vertical streaks—great camouflage when perched close to a tree trunk.

Disk of feathers around the face helps to funnel sound to the ears located underneath.

Wing feathers have soft edges so that flight is silent and won't scare off a potential meal.

HABITAT & RANGE

Barred Owls live in forests with large trees and lots of them. They are especially common in forested river bottoms and southern swamps, but they also reside in wooded suburbs and even in large city parks. Barred Owls nest in a natural tree cavity or reuse the open nest of another large bird such as a hawk or crow. These birds don't migrate, but their range is expanding.

RANGE MAP KEY

◻ YEAR-ROUND

OWL WARS

The population of Spotted Owls (left) that lives in the Pacific Northwest is protected by the Endangered Species Act. Protecting the Spotted Owls' old-growth forest habitat from being logged may not be enough, however. Turns out that Barred Owls—the Spotted Owl's closest relatives—have been moving into the area for decades and are driving out the less aggressive Spotted Owls. Should people intervene or should we let nature take its course? There don't seem to be any easy answers.

Mini-Profiles

SOUTHERN SWAMP AND BAYOU

Few people live in swamps, but for many birds, a swamp is a paradise full of food and a safe place to nest and raise a family. These birds may not be easy to spot, but keep your eyes peeled—you never know what you'll see.

PIED-BILLED GREBE

SCIENTIFIC NAME: *Podilymbus podiceps*
LENGTH: 13½ in (34 cm)
WINGSPAN: 16 in (41 cm)

In the U.S., Pied-billed Grebes live in watery places from Maine to California, but they are especially common in southern swamps and lakes. In winter, there are more Pied-billed Grebes in the South because birds that breed farther north migrate south. The Pied-billed Grebe looks and acts like an odd type of duck. However, unlike a duck, which uses its webbed feet to swim, all grebes have separate toes with flaps of skin on either side to propel it through the water. Although the Pied-billed Grebe is a good flyer, it prefers to swim. It dives underwater to catch its prey—crayfish, aquatic insects, and fish.

PURPLE GALLINULE

SCIENTIFIC NAME: *Porphyrio martinica*
LENGTH: 13 in (33 cm)
WINGSPAN: 22 in (56 cm)

The brightly colored Purple Gallinule is nicknamed the "Southern Lily Pad Chicken" or the "Swamp Hen" because of its size and shape—not because it is related to the kind of chickens that are on our dinner tables. Long yellow legs that end in very long and slender toes allow the Purple Gallinule to stride across the vegetation-covered surface of a pond or swampy area while searching for food. An omnivore, it will eat the leaves, seeds, and fruits of a variety of plants growing in the water or on land; it also devours insects, snakes, frogs, spiders, worms, and fish, and the eggs and young of other birds. Newly hatched chicks are fed by their parents as well as by up to eight "helpers" who are usually the older siblings.

YELLOW-CROWNED NIGHT-HERON

SCIENTIFIC NAME: *Nyctanassa violacea*
LENGTH: 24 in (61 cm)
WINGSPAN: 42 in (107 cm)

Yellow-crowned Night-Herons have a favorite food—crabs, which they hunt with slow, stalking movements in the swampy wetlands, marshes, and bayous where they live. When a large crab is caught, the Yellow-crowned Night-Heron slowly tears it apart and devours it, body first. The two species are so tied together that the timing of the Yellow-crowned's breeding cycle is determined by the availability of enough crabs, although the secretive Yellow-crowned also eats crayfish, insects, small fish, and frogs, when living in inland freshwater locations.

SWALLOW-TAILED KITE

SCIENTIFIC NAME: *Elanoides forficatus*
LENGTH: 23 in (58 cm)
WINGSPAN: 48 in (122 cm)

One of the most graceful fliers in the bird world, the Swallow-tailed Kite soars high on rising hot air (called a thermal), swoops low in a stiff breeze, and cruises over tree-filled swamps and bayous, all while searching for large flying insects to snatch up and eat on the wing. It also drops down on snakes, lizards, and frogs. The Swallow-tailed Kite has a white head and belly, black back and wings, and a long forked tail that moves constantly in flight, helping to make turns and maneuver in the sky. It breeds along the Gulf Coast, in Florida, and as far north as South Carolina; it winters in South America.

PILEATED WOODPECKER

SCIENTIFIC NAME: *Dryocopus pileatus*
LENGTH: 16½ in (42 cm)
WINGSPAN: 29 in (74 cm)

If you see a huge, red-crested, black-and-white bird that makes your jaw drop in amazement, you are undoubtedly looking at a Pileated (PILL-ee-ay-ted) Woodpecker. The size of a crow, the Pileated is the biggest woodpecker in North America. A very loud drumming sound means the Pileated is drilling into a big tree or a fallen log in search of beetles and carpenter ants. Its call is a loud, piercing *kee-kee-kee.* Pileated Woodpeckers are most common in the dark, swampy forests of the Deep South, but also live throughout the eastern half of the U.S. and in the Pacific Northwest.

PROTHONOTARY WARBLER

SCIENTIFIC NAME: *Protonotaria citrea*
LENGTH: 5½ in (14 cm)
WINGSPAN: 8¾ in (22 cm)

A small bird with a very long name, the Prothonotary Warbler is a brilliant, golden-yellow spot of color in its dark, swampy home. The species got its name from the resemblance of its bright yellow plumage to the colorful robes worn by Vatican clerks (prothonotaries) who serve the pope. The Prothonotary is the only eastern wood-warbler that nests in tree cavities—often holes carved out by Downy Woodpeckers—or nesting boxes. Loss of habitat puts the Prothonotary Warbler at risk, both in its U.S. breeding grounds and in the Central and South American mangrove swamps where it spends the winter.

River
and Marsh

BLACK-CROWNED NIGHT-HERON

River and Marsh

HABITAT

GREAT BLUE HERON

COMMON
YELLOWTHROAT

RICH WITH WILDLIFE

Wherever you are, a river is probably not far away. Rivers can be huge watery highways, like the Mississippi or the Colorado, or they can be a summertime trickle that turns into a torrent in the spring. A marsh is a waterlogged area where grasses or reeds grow, but not many trees. Marshes are often found next to rivers and lakes. These freshwater areas are rich with wildlife of all kinds—from microscopic animals to predators such as Bald Eagles and river otters.

BALD EAGLE

BELTED KINGFISHER

RED-WINGED
BLACKBIRD

127

Great Blue Heron

THE LONG-LEGGED, MAJESTIC Great Blue Heron is the largest heron in North America, and can be found in wetland areas everywhere in the lower 48 states and much of Canada. The Great Blue is a patient hunter. It often stands motionless for long stretches of time waiting for a frog, fish, or snake to wander within range. Then, with lightning speed, its long neck propels its dagger-like bill toward the water to snatch up a meal. The catch is first subdued and then swallowed headfirst. Striding majestically through shallow water, or taking off with slow, powerful wing beats, its long legs trailing behind, the Great Blue Heron is an awe-inspiring sight. The heron's powerful wings measure six feet (1.8 m) from tip to tip.

SCIENTIFIC NAME: *Ardea herodias*
LENGTH: 46 in (117 cm)
WINGSPAN: 72 in (183 cm)

VITAL STATISTICS

VOICE

When arriving at their nest, Great Blues greet each other with a squawking *roh-roh-roh*. If the birds are disturbed, a clucking *go-go-go* builds to a loud *frawnk*, and the whole performance can last as long as 20 seconds. When threatened, Great Blues let loose with an ear-shattering *FRAWNK!* This call may be the reason some people know this bird as "Big Cranky."

FOOD

Great Blue Herons eat just about anything they can catch in or near the water, including fish, frogs, snakes, lizards, insects, and small mammals. They grab small prey in their strong bills and sometimes spear larger fish with the bill's daggerlike tip. Great Blues also hunt for rodents in grasslands and farm fields.

HABITAT & RANGE

Great Blue Herons live in both freshwater and saltwater environments. In the Northeast, they have benefited from an increase in the number of beavers. Beavers build dams across streams and along river edges that create ponds that are ideal hunting grounds. Their

TO KEEP its balance in flight, the Great Blue—like all herons—folds its neck into a compact **S-shape** and tucks it in close to its body while its long legs trail out behind.

A CLOSER LOOK

Pointed bill is used to grab prey, but usually not to stab it.

Breeding bird has ornate plumes on the head and hanging off the neck and back.

S-shaped neck is hinged in the middle to allow it to jab forward at its prey.

The color of its body is gray, even though its name says "blue."

Long, black legs allow wading in deep water where smaller herons can't go.

nesting areas are often located in swamps, on islands, or near lakes and ponds surrounded by forests. Great Blues that nest in Canada migrate south for the winter.

RANGE MAP KEY

- SUMMER (breeding)
- WINTER (nonbreeding)
- YEAR-ROUND

LOOKING GOOD

Not many people know the Great Blue's secret to good grooming: It carries a comb wherever it goes. The claw on the middle toe of each foot has special comblike teeth growing from it that are used for scratching and preening its handsome feathers. For an added touch, special feathers on its chest grow continually and produce "powder down" that is used to clean off swamp goo and fish slime.

Bald Eagle

THE BALD EAGLE became the United States' national emblem in 1782. This majestic bird's favorite food is fish, and flying low over the water, it will nab a large fish swimming near the surface in its talons or even wade into shallow water to grab one. In addition to being a fierce predator, it is also a thief and a scavenger. Rather than do its own fishing, it is more likely to attack an Osprey and steal its catch, or feed on dead fish or other carrion it finds on a riverbank. By the mid-1900s, Bald Eagles were seriously endangered because of hunting and pesticide pollution (such as DDT). Thanks to the efforts of conservationists, special protections were put in place. Today the Bald Eagle is thriving and can be found all across North America.

SCIENTIFIC NAME: *Haliaeetus leucocephalus*
LENGTH: 34 in (86 cm)
WINGSPAN: 80 in (203 cm)

VOICE

For such a large, powerful bird, the Bald Eagle has a surprisingly high-pitched voice and weak twittering call of *kwit kwit kee-kee-kee-kee-keer*.

FOOD

When they are available, fish are pretty much all that Bald Eagles eat. It takes time for an eagle to become an expert fish-catcher, so young birds are more likely to look for dead fish or try to steal a meal. When fish are scarce, eagles will hunt reptiles, turtles, frogs, shellfish, small mammals such as squirrels, and large birds like ducks or coots. Bald Eagles sometimes hunt together but are much more likely to steal food from each other than to share.

HABITAT & RANGE

Bald Eagles usually live near lakes, reservoirs, rivers, marshes, swamps, and seacoasts. They are also occasionally found in open, dry country or on mountaintops. In winter, large numbers of eagles gather to feed at garbage dumps, fish processing plants, near dams, and below hydroelectric plants, where fish are killed by passing through the water intakes.

IT TAKES about **five** years for a young Bald Eagle to reach adulthood and get a completely white head and tail.

A CLOSER LOOK

Only the adult has a white head and tail. Young eagles have brown heads and tails.

Huge yellow bill, hooked at the tip for tearing apart its prey

Heavy brown body

Large, very sharp talons for killing prey and carrying it off

Adult

They build huge nests of sticks, high up in a tree, often building on top of a previous year's nest. One nest in Ohio was used for 34 years and weighed more than two tons (1.8 t). Bald Eagles are most abundant in Alaska. In winter, many eagles gather along the Mississippi and Missouri Rivers.

RANGE MAP KEY

SUMMER (breeding)

WINTER (nonbreeding)

MIGRATION

YEAR-ROUND

WINTERTIME IS VACATION TIME

During the winter months, eagles are likely to be found hanging out with other eagles in locations with lots of easy-to-obtain food. They don't really do much. A group of eagles studied in Washington State spent 98 percent of their time either perched or roosting (sleeping), and only 2 percent flying or feeding. By comparison, the spring and summer months are exhausting, with courtship, mating, nest-building, and hunting down enough food for a family of hungry, growing eaglets.

Belted Kingfisher

WHEN EXCITED OR FEELING threatened, the Belted Kingfisher raises its shaggy crest feathers, spreads its wings, and poses in ways that show off its large bill. Unlike many species of birds, the female kingfisher is more colorful than the male. True to its name, this bird is great at catching fish. Studying the water from an overhanging perch, the kingfisher spots its prey. Then, after a short flight or brief hover overhead, it dives headfirst into the water and grabs the fish with its bill. It then slams the fish against a branch to kill it, before swallowing it whole. Young birds are taught how to fish by their parents, who drop dead fish in the water for their young to practice on.

SCIENTIFIC NAME: *Megaceryle alcyon*
LENGTH: 13 in (33 cm)
WINGSPAN: 20 in (51 cm)

VITAL STATISTICS

VOICE

All kingfishers are members of the same family as the Laughing Kookaburra of Australia. Although not quite as loud as a kookaburra, these alert and highly territorial birds announce their presence to all comers with a loud, staccato rattle-call, heard year-round and often given in flight.

FOOD

Small fish, four to five inches (10 to 13 cm) long or less, make up most of the Belted Kingfisher's diet, which also includes crayfish, frogs, tadpoles, and insects. It hunts by hovering or from a perch overlooking clear waterways—it needs clear water in order to see its prey swimming below the surface. The parts of its prey that it can't digest—mostly scales and bones—get coughed up later as a pellet.

HABITAT & RANGE

Belted Kingfishers are found all across the country near rivers, streams, lakes, ponds, and estuaries with clear water and an abundance of fish. For nesting, they search for a nearby steep riverbank or gravel pit. There they dig a tunnel-like burrow that extends several feet or more into the bank. Birds that breed in the north migrate south in winter when rivers and lakes freeze over.

WHEN plunging headfirst into the water, the Belted Kingfisher sometimes submerges its **whole body** underwater.

A CLOSER LOOK

When a kingfisher is agitated its crest is held straight up.

Female

Male

The male kingfisher has a single blue "belt" and the female has two, one blue and one rust-colored.

Tiny feet and short legs are good for perching and shuffling through the nest tunnel.

The large bill is used to grab a fish and also to subdue it.

RANGE MAP KEY

SUMMER (breeding)

WINTER (nonbreeding)

YEAR-ROUND

A WATERY KINGDOM

What matters most to a kingfisher is a good extent of clear water with lots of fish and a nearby dirt bank to dig a nest tunnel into. So, unlike most birds, a pair of kingfishers defends a stretch of water, not a plot of land. Their home territory is usually about a half mile (0.8 km) of river or lakeshore from which all other kingfishers are chased off.

Common Yellowthroat

SCIENTIFIC NAME: *Geothlypis trichas*
LENGTH: 5 in (13 cm)
WINGSPAN: 6¾ in (17 cm)

THE COMMON YELLOWTHROAT is one of a group of colorful birds called warblers. In the U.S. and Canada there are over 60 species of warblers. These small birds usually stay hidden in underbrush or high up in trees so they can be hard to spot. Many bird-watchers say that warblers are their favorite group of birds. The Common Yellowthroat is a common warbler and in summer it lives across the U.S. and Canada. The male's black bandit mask and bright yellow throat are unique and make it easy to identify. From spring through fall, look for it near the ground in any marshy area with cattails or reeds. While you're looking, you may see other warblers too.

VITAL STATISTICS

VOICE

The male Common Yellowthroat sings a loud song that sounds like *witchity witchity witchity witchity wich*. You will hear his song more often than you will see him. He usually sings while hidden in the marsh. (See the bottom of this page for a birding trick that might help.) Both the male and the female give the same call, a loud, husky *tschep* and make rapid chattering noises.

FOOD

Yellowthroats eat lots of spiders. But besides this first choice, insects of many different types are eaten. Food is found by searching through the reeds and underbrush. Sometimes flying insects are pursued and captured in the air.

HABITAT & RANGE

Yellowthroats live in marshes and areas with tangled vegetation such as overgrown fields, willow thickets, and dense patches of wild berries. These warbles breed in almost every U.S. state and Canadian province, and also in Mexico. In fall most birds

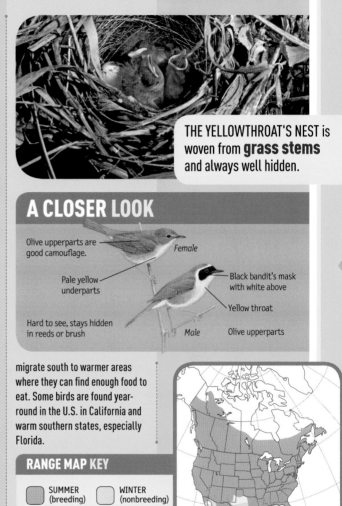

THE YELLOWTHROAT'S NEST is woven from **grass stems** and always well hidden.

A CLOSER LOOK

Olive upperparts are good camouflage.

Female

Pale yellow underparts

Black bandit's mask with white above

Yellow throat

Hard to see, stays hidden in reeds or brush

Male

Olive upperparts

migrate south to warmer areas where they can find enough food to eat. Some birds are found year-round in the U.S. in California and warm southern states, especially Florida.

RANGE MAP KEY

SUMMER (breeding)	WINTER (nonbreeding)
MIGRATION	YEAR-ROUND

TO SEE A YELLOWTHROAT...TRY PISHING

Warblers can be hard to see, but birders have a trick that often lures them into view—pishing. It's not what it sounds like; it's a mouth noise that attracts small birds. Here's how to do it: Keep your mouth almost closed and make the sound *pish* quickly and over and over by just moving your lips open and closed: *pish-pish-pish-pish-pish-pish*. Stand near a place you think a bird may be hiding and give it a try. Stop and listen for a response and look for movement. Keep trying.

Red-winged Blackbird

THE RED-WINGED BLACKBIRD is one of the most abundant birds in North America. In early spring, males arrive back at their breeding marshes before the females and immediately start singing, flashing their vivid red shoulders, and claiming territory. The most aggressive, loudest, and flashiest male may attract up to 15 females. The females, which look a bit like streaky sparrows, take on most of the parenting duties. While the female is building a nest and later on incubating her eggs, the male Red-wing spends much of the day defending his territory from other males, nest predators (crows, hawks, snakes), and even people or livestock. Sometimes Red-wing males will band together to drive a large intruder away.

SCIENTIFIC NAME: *Agelaius phoeniceus*
LENGTH: 8¾ in (22 cm)
WINGSPAN: 13 in (33 cm)

VITAL STATISTICS

VOICE

For many people, the male Red-winged Blackbird's liquid gurgling call—*konk-la-ree!* ending in a trill—is a signal that spring has begun, even if there is still snow on the ground and ice in the streams and marshes. Their most common call is a flat *chack*.

FOOD

In the summer, Red-wings eat a mixed diet of insects, seeds, and berries. During the winter, they eat seeds and grains, like corn and wheat, often feeding in huge flocks in farm fields. They will also visit bird feeders, where millet and corn are their favorite foods.

HABITAT & RANGE

Colonies of Red-winged Blackbirds nest in marshes, saltwater wetlands, riverside reed beds, roadside ditches, and suburban ponds if there are cattails growing at the edges. In winter, large numbers of Red-wings flock together and join up with other "black birds," such as grackles, cowbirds, and starlings. These winter flocks—sometimes with more than a million birds in them—gather in farm fields, livestock feedlots, marshes, and even in suburban neighborhoods. They begin to migrate as early as February and also live in Mexico and Central America.

RED-WINGED Blackbird nests are woven around an **upright** marsh plant and take females about **five** days to build.

A CLOSER LOOK

The female is brownish overall with streaks on the belly and a pale stripe over the eye.

Females

The male is glossy black with brilliant red and yellow shoulder patches (called "epaulets").

The sharply pointed bill is good for grabbing insects and seeds, and it can also be inserted into a likely spot and forcibly opened to expose hidden prey.

Male

RANGE MAP KEY

- SUMMER (breeding)
- WINTER (nonbreeding)
- YEAR-ROUND

THE RED BADGE OF COURAGE

Male Red-wings establish a breeding territory by singing and displaying the red epaulet feathers on their wings. These feathers can be raised, and when the shoulders are thrust outward, they blaze bright crimson in the sun; below the red is a line of yellow feathers. Higher perches make for a better show and are an indication of a male's dominance. If a weaker male is trespassing on another male's territory or wants to sneak through the marsh, he can hide his red shoulder patches to avoid being attacked by a more aggressive male.

Mini-Profiles

RIVER AND MARSH

Rivers are great places to see birds as they fly across open areas or feed along the shoreline. If you're planning a boating trip or just strolling by a river or marshland, see if you can spot these birds.

CANADA GOOSE

SCIENTIFIC NAME: *Branta canadensis*
LENGTH: 40 in (102 cm)
WINGSPAN: 55 in (140 cm)

Most people are familiar with the Canada Goose—brown body, long black neck, and white "chinstrap"—but did you know that during the past 50 years, many Canada Geese have stopped migrating to Canada? Large numbers have taken up year-round residence in city parks, reservoirs, riverbanks, ponds, airports, and golf courses all over North America. They graze on grass and a variety of pond and river plants. Their call is a nasal *honk-a-lonk* or two-syllable *ka-ronk*. Some Canada Geese still migrate in spring and fall.

SANDHILL CRANE

SCIENTIFIC NAME: *Antigone canadensis*
LENGTH: 46 in (117 cm)
WINGSPAN: 77 in (196 cm)

The Sandhill Crane is a big gray bird that can be mistaken for a Great Blue Heron (see pp. 128–129). Cranes nest in freshwater marshes in the Northwest, upper Great Lakes, and Canada, and spend the winter months farther south, from California to Florida. There are only 15 species of cranes in the world and most of them are endangered. The Sandhill Crane is one of the few that is doing well. In early spring, about half a million cranes gather along the Platte River in Nebraska before flying north to their breeding areas.

DOUBLE-CRESTED CORMORANT

SCIENTIFIC NAME: *Phalacrocorax auritus*
LENGTH: 32 in (81 cm)
WINGSPAN: 52 in (132 cm)

This big, black, fish-eating bird is often seen perched on a riverbank or coastal pier with its wings held open to dry in the sun. Many waterbirds, such as ducks and geese, have waterproof feathers, but not the cormorant —its feathers can get soaked. This makes it easier for the cormorant to dive underwater and chase after fish, but it's not good for flying or staying warm. When the cormorant is swimming, sometimes all that is visible is its long, S-shaped neck and orange face. Cormorants nest in colonies and build big, bulky nests made of sticks.

BLACK-CROWNED NIGHT-HERON

SCIENTIFIC NAME: *Nycticorax nycticorax*
LENGTH: 25 in (64 cm)
WINGSPAN: 44 in (112 cm)

If their nesting colony is disturbed, the young Black-crowned Night-Herons will poop and puke on the intruder. Their strategy must work—the Black-crowned is the most widely distributed heron in the world. Nesting colonies are located in trees near marshes, riversides, and swamps across the U.S. The adult is a short-legged heron with a gray body and black cap and back; young birds are brown and spotted with white. True to its name, the Black-crowned Night-Heron feeds mainly at dusk and during the night.

AMERICAN COOT

SCIENTIFIC NAME: *Fulica americana*
LENGTH: 15½ in (39 cm)
WINGSPAN: 24 in (61 cm)

If you're visiting a marsh and hear loud cackling, grunting, and croaking calls, don't be alarmed—it's probably some American Coots having a disagreement. American Coots are noisy, quarrelsome birds that don't like company when they are nesting. They are plump, dark gray waterbirds with white bills. They have toes with flaps of skin (lobes) on either side to assist in swimming. For food they eat water plants and hunt for snails, small fish, and crayfish. These birds nest in freshwater marshes and are very common across most of North America.

YELLOW WARBLER

SCIENTIFIC NAME: *Setophaga petechia*
LENGTH: 5 in (13 cm)
WINGSPAN: 8 in (20 cm)

The bright, butter-colored Yellow Warbler is a small songbird that nests in North America and migrates to Central and South America for the winter. For some, this includes a nonstop flight across the Gulf of Mexico, a feat of amazing endurance given its tiny size. In summer, Yellow Warblers nest in willows and thickets alongside rivers, streams, and marshes across much of the United States and Canada and eat insects, such as caterpillars, midges, and leafhoppers. Sometimes a female Brown-headed Cowbird will sneak into a warbler's nest and lay her own eggs there.

Prairie and Plains

RED-TAILED HAWK

Prairie and Plains

HABITAT

WESTERN MEADOWLARK

KILLDEER

HOME ON THE RANGE

The great midsection of the United States was once a vast rolling sea of wild grass with an abundance of animals and birds. Huge herds of buffalo migrated across the prairie, which they shared with abundant deer, elk, and antelope. Today, most of the once wild prairie has been converted to farmland and the remaining buffalo are mostly found in national parks. Millions of wild birds, however, still migrate across the region, nest and breed there in the summer, or live there year-round.

WESTERN KINGBIRD

RED-TAILED HAWK

BLACK-BILLED MAGPIE

Killdeer

THE KILLDEER IS A SHOREBIRD, but it doesn't live by the seashore. It prefers mudflats, short-grass fields, and gravel bars. Where humans live, it is equally fond of construction sites, gravel rooftops, lawns, pastures, and golf courses. Look for it out in the open. The Killdeer has long legs and is often seen running in a herky-jerky motion, stopping frequently to peck at the ground for food. Killdeer are also active at night. Have you ever been awake in the middle of the night and heard a loud and mysterious cry *kill-dee kill-dee kill-dee?* That was a Killdeer flying overhead, perhaps on a moonlit night. In the daylight, its two black breast bands, white forehead, and long tail make it easy to identify.

SCIENTIFIC NAME: *Charadrius vociferus*
LENGTH: 10½ in (27 cm)
WINGSPAN: 24 in (61 cm)

VOICE

The Killdeer makes a large variety of sounds. Its most well-known call is a loud, piercing *kill-dee* that explains how it got its name. Used by the Killdeer to signal an alarm, it is often given as the bird takes flight.

FOOD

Earthworms, beetles, grasshoppers, and small seeds are among the items on the Killdeer's menu. When searching for food, its typical behavior is to run, stop, look around for something to eat, and then run again.

HABITAT & RANGE

Killdeer live all across North and Central America, and in parts of South America. They prefer flat open areas and avoid forests and mountains. Killdeer can withstand cold temperatures, but most birds that breed in Canada and the northern U.S. migrate south in the fall. Some birds travel to Mexico and the West Indies, but most migrate no farther than to the southern half of the U.S. In winter they sometimes

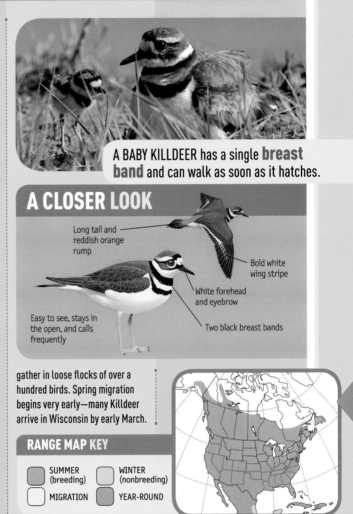

A BABY KILLDEER has a single **breast band** and can walk as soon as it hatches.

A CLOSER LOOK

Long tail and reddish orange rump

Bold white wing stripe

White forehead and eyebrow

Easy to see, stays in the open, and calls frequently

Two black breast bands

gather in loose flocks of over a hundred birds. Spring migration begins very early—many Killdeer arrive in Wisconsin by early March.

RANGE MAP KEY

- SUMMER (breeding)
- WINTER (nonbreeding)
- MIGRATION
- YEAR-ROUND

OH NO, I HAVE A BROKEN WING! JUST KIDDING.

When a Killdeer calls out loudly, spreads its tail, and drags one of its wings on the ground, it's not looking for sympathy. It's playing a deadly serious game. This is the Killdeer's "broken wing" display, used to lure a predator away from its nest on the ground. The nest is likely full of eggs or flightless baby birds. The predator, possibly a fox or coyote, follows the parent bird, thinking that an injured bird will be easy to catch. When it's far enough away from its nest the Killdeer miraculously "heals" and flies off, leaving behind a very confused predator.

Red-tailed Hawk

THE RED-TAILED HAWK—the most common hawk in North America, with a global population of about two million birds—is also one of the easiest to see. Driving through open country, you'll probably see this bulky, broad-winged hawk soaring over fields, showing its rusty red tail feathers. It perches in the open and is often seen sitting atop roadside utility poles or fence posts. Red-tails build their nests at the top of tall trees, saguaro cacti, power line towers, or on a cliff ledge. In 1992 a male Red-tailed Hawk, known to his fans as "Pale Male," began nesting with his mate on the stone ledge of an apartment building in New York City. He has nested in the same area for more than 20 years. (Wild Red-tails can live for more than 30 years.)

SCIENTIFIC NAME: *Buteo jamaicensis*
LENGTH: 22 in (56 cm)
WINGSPAN: 50 in (127 cm)

VITAL STATISTICS

VOICE

Red-tailed Hawks have a distinctive call, especially when they are flying—a harsh, descending *keee-eerrrrrr*. Their call can often be heard in the background of a film or television show set in the Old West.

FOOD

Red-tailed Hawks often hunt by sitting on a perch high up that allows them to survey the area below. They also hunt by cruising over open areas or soaring high in the air. Favorite prey includes small mammals such as mice, moles, rabbits, and voles. In the West, they seek out ground squirrels and jackrabbits. They also eat reptiles and larger birds. Most prey is captured and killed on the ground, then carried to a feeding perch to be eaten.

HABITAT & RANGE

Red-tailed Hawks live in various habitats, from mountains and woodlands to prairies and deserts, as well as city and suburban areas that have trees and open space. The Great Plains is a great place to see them soaring over the prairie.

JUVENILES have brown tails with numerous dark **bars** and are more streaked underneath.

A CLOSER LOOK

Juvenile   *Adult*

Hooked bill is used for tearing apart its prey.

Long, broad wings are perfect for soaring high in the sky.

Large, dark eyes can spot small animals from great distances. Juveniles have yellow eyes.

The "red" tail of the adult is really more of a rusty brown color.

In fall, most of the Red-tails that nested in Canada migrate to the United States. In many places, they are year-round residents.

RANGE MAP KEY

- SUMMER (breeding)
- WINTER (nonbreeding)
- YEAR-ROUND

SKY-DANCING

Courting Red-tails have some great aerial dance moves that help them bond with each other. Typically, both birds start off by soaring in wide circles at high altitudes and then the male starts showing off. Upon gaining altitude, he dives steeply, pulls out of the dive, and shoots upward. After repeating this several times, he approaches the female from above and extends his legs to touch her, then the birds may grasp one another's beaks or interlock talons and spiral toward the ground. Sometimes these aerial acrobatics include courtship feeding, with the male passing food to the female. And, of course, the whole affair is accompanied by piercing screams from both parties.

Western Kingbird

THE WESTERN KINGBIRD is a summer bird over most of the Great Plains and the western states. "Here I am! Look at me!" the handsome kingbird seems to be saying as it sits on a prominent perch, for all to see. Often found where people live, they may perch low on a fence post or barbed wire or higher up on utility wires. A curious courtship display is called the "Tumble Flight," during which the male flies to a height of about 50 feet (15.2 m), then turns sharply and begins a tumbling descent full of twists and flips accompanied with loud vocalizations. For its nest, the kingbird builds a bulky construction of twigs, bark, and rootlets, which is lined with various soft fibers.

SCIENTIFIC NAME: *Tyrannus verticalis*
LENGTH: 8¾ in (22 cm)
WINGSPAN: 15½ in (39 cm)

VOICE

The Western Kingbird's song is a fast, squeaky *pik pik peek PEEK-a-loo*. The common call is a sharp *kip*, given singly or in a stuttering series.

FOOD

Western Kingbirds feed on insects. Most prey is captured during flights from a perch (called "sallies"). Aerial pursuits sometimes take twisting, acrobatic turns as the bird follows a flying insect. Kingbirds also catch insects on the ground or pluck them off bushes. Late in the summer and in the fall, they add fruit to their diet.

HABITAT & RANGE

Western Kingbirds are summer residents from the Great Plains and west to California. They prefer dry country interspersed with trees—grasslands, foothills, farmland, and ranchland, as well as towns and urban parks. They construct their nests on the outer branches of a tree or shrub or on man-made structures such as a building, a utility pole, or even a city lamppost or backyard basketball hoop, braced against the backboard. They spend winters mainly in Mexico and Central America, and a few birds wander to the East Coast every fall.

THE WESTERN Kingbird's bill can catch large **insects,** such as grasshoppers and dragonflies.

A CLOSER LOOK

Adult's red-orange crown is kept hidden, unless the bird gets really irritated.

Pale tones and earthy colors of its feathers blend in with the colors of the prairie.

Yellow belly and blackish tail with white edges

Kingbirds (and all flycatchers) have tiny feet that are useful only for perching on small branches, wires, or posts.

RANGE MAP KEY

- SUMMER (breeding)
- WINTER (nonbreeding)
- MIGRATION

KING OF THE PRAIRIE

The Western Kingbird likes a perch with a good view. Any insect that flies by is easily picked off, but that's not the only reason. This kingbird is also on the lookout for trespassers—no matter how big. Any hawk, eagle, crow, or raven that gets too near its nest tree is relentlessly chased and pecked. Sometimes the kingbird even lands on the bigger bird's back! Being such an agile flier, the kingbird is in little danger of getting caught and it isn't long before the intruder changes course, glad to be rid of the fearless smaller bird with a big attitude.

Black-billed Magpie

THE INQUISITIVE Black-billed Magpie is easy to spot in many open spaces in the West because of its showy black-and-white plumage and extremely long tail. Magpies, in the same family as crows and jays, exhibit many fascinating behaviors. They'll follow a coyote to steal its food—one bird sneaks up behind the coyote and pulls its tail, and when it turns toward the offending bird, another magpie in the group steals the food. They also conduct "funerals" where birds will gather in a noisy flock around a dead magpie for 10 to 15 minutes and then all fly off in silence. Magpies hop and walk on the ground with a confident swagger and fly with steady, rowing wing beats often ending with a swooping glide to a perch.

SCIENTIFIC NAME: *Pica hudsonia*
LENGTH: 19 in (48 cm)
WINGSPAN: 25 in (64 cm)

VITAL STATISTICS

VOICE

Magpies have a variety of different calls including a quick series of *mag, mag, mag* and a whining, rising *mee-aaah*.

FOOD

Magpies are omnivores. They eat animal matter, either from scavenged carrion and human garbage or from animals they catch and kill—rodents, reptiles, insects, ticks (picked off live deer and moose), newly hatched baby birds, or bird eggs. They also eat large amounts of grain and fruit. They forage on the ground, rarely in trees. Magpies often hide stashes of excess food in different locations.

HABITAT & RANGE

The Black-billed Magpie is a year-round resident of prairies, scrublands, and rangelands, often near a stream, lake, or pond. Magpies are also at home in suburbs, towns, and urban parks. A magpie's nest in a tree or tall shrub is often quite noticeable—a bulky, ball-shaped construction of sticks that has an inside cup lined with mud, dung, and animal hair.

IN FLIGHT, the flashing **white** wing patches and two racing stripes on the back are hard to miss.

A CLOSER LOOK

From a distance a magpie looks black and white, but close up the black feathers glitter with blue, green, and purple colors, especially on the wings and tail.

White wing tips are hidden when the bird is perched but are flashed during aggressive displays.

Strong bill is capable of catching and killing small animals, such as rodents.

Magpies walk on the ground and have strong legs and feet.

The tail is almost as long as the body and allows it to make quick changes in flight direction. Males with longer tails are preferred by females.

Magpies don't migrate, even the ones that live as far north as Alaska.

RANGE MAP KEY

YEAR-ROUND

WHAT'S YOURS IS MINE

Magpies don't have much use for property rights. Long before Columbus visited the New World, magpies were following bison-hunting Native Americans and living on the leftovers of their hunts. When the Lewis and Clark expedition first encountered magpies in 1804 in South Dakota, the birds showed no fear of man and boldly entered their tents to steal meat.

Western Meadowlark

THE YELLOW-BREASTED Western Meadowlark is a colorful member of the blackbird family. The male sings his cheerful song all across the western United States. However, what to our ears is sweet music is serious business to the meadowlark—his song tells other meadowlarks to keep away.

SCIENTIFIC NAME: *Sturnella neglecta*
LENGTH: 9½ in (24 cm)
WINGSPAN: 14½ in (37 cm)

Any trespassing males are vigorously chased until they leave the area. If an intruder resists, he may be attacked. In the Great Plains and upper Midwest, the Western Meadowlark's range overlaps that of the closely related Eastern Meadowlark. Even though the two species look very similar, they sing different songs and don't interbreed. Meriwether Lewis was the first to point out the subtle differences between the meadowlarks in 1805.

VITAL STATISTICS

VOICE

The male Western Meadowlark usually sings his song from a prominent perch like a fence post or the top of an isolated bush. The loud, bubbly song is a burst of flute-like whistles, *tuuu-weet-too-tweed-lo-oo.*

FOOD

During the summer, meadowlarks eat insects, especially grasshoppers and crickets. In fall and winter, when there are few insects to be found, their diet is mostly weed seeds and grain.

HABITAT & RANGE

The Western Meadowlark inhabits dry rangelands, native grasslands, roadsides, large pastures, desert grasslands, and, in winter, other open areas such as croplands, feedlots, and large lawns. The female builds her nest on the ground in tall grass. The nest is a cup of grass with a domed roof woven into the grass around it. The entrance to this snug little home is a tunnel located on one side. Some birds migrate south, but birds can survive cold winters if the ground isn't

THE yellow breast and black V are more than pretty decoration; males with the brightest colors are preferred by females and **control** the best territories.

A CLOSER LOOK

Uses its sharply pointed bill to probe into the ground for insects

The brown and tan stripes on the upperparts are good camouflage, protecting birds from being spotted by a hawk flying overhead.

Adult

White outer tail feathers are hidden except when the bird flies or twitches its tail.

Juvenile

completely snow-covered. Western Meadowlarks also live in Mexico.

RANGE MAP KEY

 SUMMER (breeding)   WINTER (nonbreeding)

MIGRATION   YEAR-ROUND

MIRROR, MIRROR ON THE WALL...

If "state bird" status is a type of popularity contest in the bird world, only the Northern Cardinal tops the Western Meadowlark. The Northern Cardinal is the state bird of seven states: Illinois, Indiana, Kentucky, North Carolina, Ohio, Virginia, and West Virginia. Close behind, the Western Meadowlark is the state bird of six states: Kansas, Montana, Nebraska, North Dakota, Oregon, and Wyoming.

SHARP-TAILED GROUSE

SCIENTIFIC NAME: *Tympanuchus phasianellus*
LENGTH: 17 in (43 cm)
WINGSPAN: 25 in (64 cm)

The chicken-size Sharp-tailed Grouse is a ground-loving bird that lives in prairie grasslands with scattered trees and also in farm fields where they eat—seeds, leaves, roots, wild fruits and nuts, and insects. This bird was an important source of food for Native Americans and the early settlers of the Great Plains and western Canada. Its name refers to the pointed tail feathers that are held high when the male does his courtship dance. Males gather on traditional dancing grounds called "leks" where they strut, bow, and do a foot-stomping stutter dance to impress females.

PRAIRIE FALCON

SCIENTIFIC NAME: *Falco mexicanus*
LENGTH: 16 in (41 cm)
WINGSPAN: 40 in (102 cm)

The Prairie Falcon hunts its prey from the sky over dry western plains, prairies, and deserts. Its quarry is varied—some falcons specialize in ground squirrels, whereas others attack larger birds like Sharp-tailed Grouse (see left). Falcons also hunt jackrabbits, small birds, lizards, and large insects. The falcon's long wings and strong muscles make it very fast in the air, and after it spots a victim it simply chases it down, grabs it with its talons, and quickly dispatches it with a bite to the neck. Prairie Falcons usually choose a cliff ledge protected by an overhanging rock for nesting and sometimes share the mountainside with a pair of Common Ravens or Golden Eagles.

BURROWING OWL

SCIENTIFIC NAME: *Athene cunicularia*
LENGTH: 9½ in (24 cm)
WINGSPAN: 21 in (53 cm)

These diminutive, somewhat comical-looking owls nest in holes in the ground in open, scrubby terrain, grasslands, golf courses, and airports. They rarely dig their own holes; instead, they take over an unused burrow of a rabbit, skunk, armadillo, or prairie dog. During the day, though well camouflaged, they can be seen sitting near the entrance to their burrow. They hunt for insects by day and small mammals at night. In the Southwest, Burrowing Owls are year-round residents; those that nest farther north migrate south in the fall. The destruction of prairie dog towns and agricultural growth have greatly decreased this owl's numbers.

SCISSOR-TAILED FLYCATCHER

SCIENTIFIC NAME: *Tyrannus forficatus*
LENGTH: 13 in (33 cm)
WINGSPAN: 15 in (38 cm)

Oklahoma's state bird was well chosen—the Scissor-tail's small breeding range is centered directly on that state. From spring through fall it's hard to miss this extra-ordinary bird that sits conspicuously on roadside fences and low shrubs, tail held tightly closed and looking like a long stick. When pursuing flying insects, the surprising tail flares open, revealing its scissorlike shape and also the bird's beautiful salmon pink belly. The summer home of the so-called Texas Bird-of-Paradise is also the center of the tornado belt. Scissor-tails migrate to Mexico and Central America for the winter months.

HORNED LARK

SCIENTIFIC NAME: *Eremophila alpestris*
LENGTH: 7 in (18 cm)
WINGSPAN: 12 in (30 cm)

The grasslands and prairies of North America have a large population of Horned Larks, but this ground-loving species also lives in Europe, North Africa, and central Asia. Regardless of where they live, they prefer barren country, dry prairies, deserts, and agricultural lands. Larks that nest on the Arctic tundra join prairie-nesting birds and form large flocks in the winter months. All Horned Larks have a black mask and bib with two black "horns" (feather tufts) growing from the top of the head. Adults eat weed and grass seeds, but they feed their young a more protein-rich diet of insects. The Horned Lark's song is a series of high-pitched, tinkling notes.

DICKCISSEL

SCIENTIFIC NAME: *Spiza americana*
LENGTH: 6¼ in (16 cm)
WINGSPAN: 9¾ in (25 cm)

Like the chickadee and the phoebe, the name Dickcissel (DIK-sis-sul) comes from the song it sings: *dick dick dick ciss ciss cissel*. About the size of a large sparrow, the Dickcissel is a very common breeding bird in grasslands, prairies, and hayfields throughout the central United States. With its yellow breast and the black bib of the male, it resembles a miniature meadowlark (see pp. 152–153), which it often has for a neighbor. Dickcissels eat seeds and insects and build their nests near the ground, hidden by tall grass. In the fall, birds migrate to Central and South America.

CACTUS WREN

Deserts

Deserts

COSTA'S HUMMINGBIRD

ELF OWL

SURPRISINGLY FULL OF LIFE

Most deserts, including those of the American Southwest, are not wastelands of endless sand dunes. The Sonoran Desert stretching from California to Arizona is full of cacti, shrubs, and even a few rivers. Birds and other animals that are adapted to the heat and dryness do more than survive there—they thrive.

HARRIS'S HAWK

CACTUS WREN

GREATER
ROADRUNNER

159

Greater Roadrunner

THE AMAZING Greater Roadrunner—the state bird of New Mexico—is a ground-dwelling member of the cuckoo family that flies only when absolutely necessary. They may not fly much, but Greater Roadrunners run at speeds up to 18 miles an hour (29 km/h) when chasing prey or escaping a predator. They are also well adapted to living in their desert environment. Although they will drink water if it is available, roadrunners can survive without drinking if they are able to consume prey with high enough moisture content. Without water, they have a lot of extra salt in their bodies, but they've solved that problem. Roadrunners have a small gland in the corner of each eye that helps to eliminate extra salt.

SCIENTIFIC NAME: *Geococcyx californianus*
LENGTH: 23 in (58 cm)
WINGSPAN: 22 in (56 cm)

VOICE

The roadrunner's primary call is a dove-like, loud *coo-coo-coo-coo* trailing off at the end. Also a sharp, loud *chuk-chuk-chuk-chuk!*

FOOD

The roadrunner's diet includes small mammals like mice and young ground squirrels, birds, insects, spiders, lizards, and snakes. Tarantulas, scorpions, centipedes, and rattlesnakes are all on the menu. Large food items are beaten repeatedly against the ground to soften them up before swallowing, and roadrunners seem to suffer no ill effects from eating venomous prey.

HABITAT & RANGE

Roadrunners live in open desert areas with some brush, like the Sonoran Desert. They can also be found in areas of Texas. Although the male helps to collect twigs to build a nest, the female actually constructs it, hiding it in a low bush or cactus. And sometimes they really do run on roads—dirt roads through the desert are good pathways through the cactus and thorny brush. Roadrunners live in the same place year-round. They are also found in Mexico.

WHEN RUNNING, the roadrunner often uses its wings and tail as rudders to **steer** with.

A CLOSER LOOK

Shiny black crest is raised when the roadrunner is on alert or agitated.

The heavy bill is long and slightly hooked at the tip.

Tail is very long and is tipped with white.

Wings are short; roadrunners don't fly very much.

Large feet and long legs for running through the desert

RANGE MAP KEY

YEAR-ROUND

STRONG MAGIC

The Hopi, and other Pueblo tribes of the Southwest, revered the roadrunner and told stories of its bravery and endurance. Roadrunners were medicine birds, and drawings of the roadrunner's X-shaped footprints were sacred symbols that could ward off evil. The footprints offered protection because they looked the same coming and going—the roadrunner's foot has two toes facing forward and two facing backward, an unusual arrangement in birds. Any dangerous spirits that were trying to follow you wouldn't know which way to go.

Costa's Hummingbird

HUMMINGBIRDS, OR "HUMMERS," as they are often known, are the smallest of all birds. The desert-dwelling Costa's Hummingbird is one of the smallest of all—it weighs less than a U.S. nickel. But don't let its size fool you—this tiny bird is a dynamo of energy and it's fearless too. The male is very ornate with glittering violet-purple feathers on his throat that flare out on either side and cover the top of his head. The female is less showy, but that makes her less obvious to predators. She is responsible for building the nest, hatching the two eggs, and caring for the young all on her own. That doesn't sound like a fair division of labor to humans, but that's the way almost all hummingbirds have evolved to live.

SCIENTIFIC NAME: *Calypte costae*
LENGTH: 3¼ in (8 cm)
WINGSPAN: 4¾ in (12 cm)

162

VITAL STATISTICS

VOICE

The Costa's Hummingbird makes some very loud sounds for such a tiny bird. Its call is a high, metallic *tink*, often given in a series, followed by a scratchy squeal. The male's song is even higher pitched and sounds like a piercing buzz.

FOOD

Like all hummingbirds, sugary flower nectar is its main food. Costa's Hummingbirds also eat tiny flying insects that they catch in flight.

HABITAT & RANGE

Costa's Hummingbirds live in deserts and other dry areas of the southwestern U.S. and western Mexico. When desert flowers disappear by late June, many Costa's Hummingbirds move toward the Pacific coast where it is not as hot and dry, and where more flowers are in bloom. Costa's Hummingbirds also breed in dry areas along the California coast, possibly raising a second family after nesting in the desert earlier in the year. In fall, some birds migrate south into Mexico and spend the winter months there.

THE BILL of a baby **hummingbird** is short when it hatches, but it grows quickly.

A CLOSER LOOK

Very small and compact, even for a hummingbird

Purple head and throat (gorget) that looks black in some light

Extra-long gorget feathers on each side

Male

Plain face and throat with a pale gray patch behind the eye

Green upperparts that glitter

Female

RANGE MAP KEY

SUMMER (breeding)

WINTER (nonbreeding)

YEAR-ROUND

SEE ME, HEAR ME

A male Costa's Hummingbird knows how to impress a female. He performs an amazing acrobatic show known as the Looping Dive-and-Whistle Display. He starts out by circling around a perched female and then flies straight up, high into the air. Then, he zooms straight back down while making a drawn-out, shrill whistle. At the bottom of his dive near the perched female, he makes an abrupt U-turn and flies straight back up to do it all again. By the time he's finished he's made four or more roller-coaster loops.

Harris's Hawk

THESE REMARKABLE raptors are best known for forming avian "wolf packs," family groups that hunt together, with each bird having a specific job. Some spread out and conceal themselves on perches, waiting patiently, while others find and flush a ground squirrel or speedy jackrabbit out into the open.

SCIENTIFIC NAME: *Parabuteo unicinctus*
LENGTH: 21 in (53 cm)
WINGSPAN: 46 in (117 cm)

When this happens, a "lookout" bird calls loudly and the fleeing prey runs right into the waiting talons of one of the hunters. The desert-dwelling Harris's Hawk is easy to identify. It has a dark brown body with beautiful chestnut inner wings and leg feathers. In flight its long black tail with a white base and a white tip is hard to miss. If you're in cactus country and you see a Harris's Hawk, look around, as there are probably more nearby.

VOICE

The Harris's Hawk has a high-pitched voice. Its calls are a series of harsh *eeeeer eeeeer eeeeer* cries.

FOOD

The Harris's Hawk's favorite prey are small to medium-size mammals like kangaroo rats, wood rats, ground squirrels, and jackrabbits; they also attack medium-size birds like quail and woodpeckers, and they eat lizards and large insects when they are abundant.

HABITAT & RANGE

Harris's Hawks like it hot. They are found mostly in saguaro cactus desert in Arizona and mesquite brush country in Texas and New Mexico. Rivers lined with cottonwoods and other types of trees and brush are also wild places where they can be found. Recently, more and more Harris's Hawks have taken up residence in the suburbs of some cities in the desert Southwest, such as Phoenix and Tucson, Arizona. Harris's Hawks are permanent residents—they do not migrate. These birds also live in Central and South America, as far south as southern Chile.

HARRIS'S Hawks often build their stick nests nestled in the arms of a large saguaro **cactus** or at the top of a tree.

A CLOSER LOOK

Long legs are useful for grabbing prey, and these hawks can run and hop surprisingly fast when chasing after a meal.

Long black tail with white tip and base; a long tail helps when making very sharp turns.

Skin on the face, legs, and toes is bright yellow.

Long black talons are used for catching prey.

RANGE MAP KEY

YEAR-ROUND

A PLACE FOR EVERYONE

Within a group of Harris's Hawks, each bird has a place in the "pecking order" and rarely challenges a bird of a higher rank. The most dominant bird is the "alpha" breeding female, followed by the "alpha" breeding male. Of lesser rank are the "beta" male helpers, followed by one to four "gamma" helpers at the bottom. "Gammas" are usually younger birds.

Elf Owl

THE ELF OWL is the tiniest owl in the world—about the size of a sparrow—and looks like a toy soldier next to its big cousin the Great Horned Owl (see pp. 74–75). Even so, these tiny desert predators have all the standard owl equipment: sharp talons, hooked beak, silent wings, nighttime vision, and sharp hearing. But, rather than hunting rats and squirrels, these owls do battle with moths and beetles every night. Elf Owls nest in an old woodpecker hole carved into a tree or saguaro cactus. Nesting in a hole helps shelter them from the hot sun, and a pair of owls may use the same nest hole for a number of years. Nest holes are valuable real estate and are vigorously defended from other hole-nesting birds.

SCIENTIFIC NAME: *Micrathene whitneyi*
LENGTH: 5¼ in (13 cm)
WINGSPAN: 13 in (33 cm)

VOICE

Despite their small size, Elf Owls sing very loud chattering songs. The sound—different from all other North American owls—has been compared to the high-pitched yipping of a puppy.

FOOD

Elf Owls eat large insects, like moths, crickets, and beetles; occasionally they'll consume scorpions, spiders, and small lizards. They usually hunt from a perch and fly out after spotting a target, but they also land on the ground and pursue prey on foot for short distances. The insect parts that Elf Owls cannot digest are coughed up in compact pellets after a few hours.

HABITAT & RANGE

In the United States, Elf Owls live in southern Arizona, southern New Mexico, and western Texas. Although they are fairly common in lowland desert areas with saguaro cactus and thorny woodlands, they also live at higher elevations in streamside forests and mountain

INSIDE a saguaro cactus, a pair of Elf Owls will raise a family of two to four tiny **owlets.** The young owls leave the nest hole as soon as they can **fly.**

A CLOSER LOOK

Large yellow eyes gather in lots of light and face forward (like your eyes) for judging distance to a target.

Large rounded head with no ear tufts

The hooked bill and large mouth is mostly hidden by feathers.

Plumage is a combination of reddish brown, gray, and white.

Wing feathers have soft edges so a flying owl makes no sound when hunting.

Big feet, for such a small bird, armed with razor-sharp talons

canyons. Sometimes migrating birds get lost, and Elf Owls have been found on oil platforms in the middle of the Gulf of Mexico. In the winter, Elf Owls live in Mexico.

RANGE MAP KEY

- SUMMER (breeding)
- WINTER (nonbreeding)
- MIGRATION
- YEAR-ROUND

ALWAYS FULL

Elf Owls are effective hunters, often catching more than they or their owlets can eat right away. The parent owls select the largest food items—sphinx moths, scorpions (with stingers removed), large beetles—and store them right in the nest with the owlets. Who knows when the craving for a juicy moth or crunchy scorpion will hit?

Cactus Wren

THE CACTUS WREN—the largest wren in North America and the state bird of Arizona—is well suited for life in the cactus-filled deserts of the Southwest. It is able to survive without a source of water, obtaining all the fluid it needs from the insects it eats or a bite of juicy cactus fruit. Pairs stay together all year and are often seen as they feed and call to each other. In late summer, entire families can be seen hopping on the ground, posturing with spread wings and tails, and generally being noisy. They often use their long bills to move fallen leaves or flip over a small rock to look for a tasty insect. Cactus Wrens also live around people in desert suburbs, especially in yards landscaped with cacti.

SCIENTIFIC NAME: *Campylorhynchus brunneicapillus*
LENGTH: 8½ in (22 cm)
WINGSPAN: 11 in (28 cm)

VOICE

Harsh and low pitched, the Cactus Wren's rapid song, *char char char char char char char*, increases in volume from beginning to end—it sounds like someone trying and failing to start an old car. All year long, even in the middle of the day when most desert birds are quiet, the wrens keep singing.

FOOD

Cactus Wrens eat insects and spiders. Their favorite foods are beetles, ants, wasps, grasshoppers, butterflies, and moths. Always on the lookout for a new food source, suburban-dwelling Cactus Wrens have discovered how to pick smashed bugs from the front grilles of parked cars.

HABITAT & RANGE

Cactus Wrens build their nests, perch, and hunt for prey amid the sharp spines of desert vegetation, most often cholla and saguaro cacti. They are also found in mesquite brush, among yucca plants, and in towns and coastal areas where cactus and thorny shrubs grows. Cactus Wrens do not migrate, and they may hatch and raise as many as three families in a single year. They also live in Mexico.

WITH the bottoms of its toes protected by tough **leathery** skin, the Cactus Wren can perch anywhere it wants to.

A CLOSER LOOK

Bill is an all-purpose tool, large enough to deal with a big caterpillar and delicate enough to pick up a tiny ant.

White stripe over the eye

Spots on the breast are variable; some birds have lots.

Streaks and bars on the back and wings are good camouflage.

Fairly long legs and strong feet for walking on the desert floor or perching on thorny plants

Tail is long and crossed with black bands.

RANGE MAP KEY

☐ YEAR-ROUND

MASTER BUILDER

Nest building is an important skill that all Cactus Wrens must learn. The complicated nest—usually nestled in the arms of a cholla cactus or other spiny plant—is a large, ball-shaped construction of sticks and weed stems. It has a central chamber lined with feathers and is connected to the outside by a short tunnel, with a convenient "doorstep" perch at the front of the tunnel. Each pair builds several bulky nests in their territory and uses them for roosting year-round. Young birds start building their own nests for nighttime roosting when about four months old.

Mini-Profiles

DESERTS

Some desert birds are easy to see as they soar overhead, but many others stay hidden among the cacti and rocks. Lots of birds call the desert home. Here are six more of them you can watch for.

GAMBEL'S QUAIL

SCIENTIFIC NAME: *Callipepla gambelii*
LENGTH: 11 in (28 cm)
WINGSPAN: 15 in (38 cm)

The Gambel's Quail is a plump, short-tailed bird of the desert Southwest with a loud, easy-to-remember call, *chi-CA-go-go*. Males and females both have a curious, comma-shaped topknot of feathers that bobs forward. Because they are tame and sociable, Gambel's have adapted well to the increasing number of people living in desert areas. They frequently come to backyards for birdseed and an essential drink of water. Out in the desert, family groups—coveys—scour the ground for seeds and insects, and often add buds, small cactus fruits, and berries to their diet.

WHITE-WINGED DOVE

SCIENTIFIC NAME: *Zenaida asiatica*
LENGTH: 11½ in (29 cm)
WINGSPAN: 19 in (48 cm)

The White-winged Dove is a common summer sight near the Mexican border, and its drawn-out hooting call—"who-cooks-for-you"—is heard throughout the day. When it flies, a large white wing patch is visible, but, when the wing is folded, only a thin white stripe is left in view. And check out this bird's amazing orange eyes surrounded by powder-blue skin—it looks like it's wearing makeup. Seeds and fruits make up its natural diet, but it also is attracted to bird feeders. White-winged Doves nest in trees and cacti, often in small colonies.

GILA WOODPECKER

SCIENTIFIC NAME: *Melanerpes uropygialis*
LENGTH: 9 in (24 cm)
WINGSPAN: 16 in (41 cm)

The zebra-striped back of the Gila Woodpecker is very noticeable as it clings to the side of a tall saguaro cactus. The tan head of the male is topped with a cap of red feathers that is absent in the female. They eat insects, supplemented with cactus fruit and mistletoe berries, and have learned how to hang onto a hummingbird feeder and lick up the sugary water. Many desert residents owe their cozy cavity homes to these industrious woodpeckers. Excavating a nest hole is a big project and both members of a woodpecker pair work on it. After all the excavating is done, the cavity has to dry out and the birds must wait for several months until the cactus grows an inner casing of fiber around the cavity—like a scab.

COMMON RAVEN

SCIENTIFIC NAME: *Corvus corax*
LENGTH: 24 in (61 cm)
WINGSPAN: 53 in (135 cm)

One of the most intelligent birds, the Common Raven is completely black, but it's much larger than a crow and also has a heavier bill and shaggy neck feathers. With long wings and a wedge-shaped tail, the raven can soar with ease and even plays games in the air, such as dropping and catching a stick or flying upside down. Ravens live in many different places, from deserts to high mountains to northern forests. Ravens eat just about anything: scavenged carrion, human garbage, small animals, large insects, baby birds, fish, and even wolf dung.

CURVE-BILLED THRASHER

SCIENTIFIC NAME: *Toxostoma curvirostre*
LENGTH: 11 in (28 cm)
WINGSPAN: 13½ in (34 cm)

The Curve-billed Thrasher is a common year-round resident found from the cactus-rich Sonoran Desert of Arizona to the brushlands of West Texas. It can be spotted calling loudly from atop a saguaro or prickly pear cactus, or even a street sign! The calls are very distinctive: a loud *whit-wheet* (in Arizona) or *whit-whit* (in Texas). If you live in a suburban desert community, this thrasher may be living in your backyard. Look for a brownish bird with a thick curved bill, long tail, and orange eyes. Eating a wide variety of insect prey, its diet is supplemented with seeds, wild berries, and cactus fruit.

BLACK-THROATED SPARROW

SCIENTIFIC NAME: *Amphispiza bilineata*
LENGTH: 5½ in (14 cm)
WINGSPAN: 7¾ in (20 cm)

The Black-throated Sparrow is a common desert bird but also somewhat of a mystery. Few ornithologists (bird scientists) have studied the Black-throated Sparrow as much as they have other sparrows, so there is much to be discovered about its habits and behavior. Bird-watchers enjoy seeing them because they are handsome and easy to identify. The large black bib and bold white face stripes give the adult a dressed-up look, but young birds are plainer and have brown streaks instead of a black bib. The Black-throated Sparrow lives in the desert Southwest and as far north as southern Idaho and west into California.

Western
Mountains

GOLDEN EAGLE

Western Mountains

WESTERN TANAGER

STELLER'S JAY

ROCKY MOUNTAIN ADVENTURE

The Rockies, a mighty spine of tall mountains, run from Canada all the way south to Mexico, dividing the Great Plains from the western states and forming the Continental Divide. Many of the highest areas are protected as public parks and forests of breathtaking beauty, where families can experience the grandeur of nature and have fun going camping, hiking, and river rafting. The Rockies are a terrific place to see wildlife, and there are lots of special birds to find on a Rocky Mountain adventure.

GOLDEN EAGLE

MOUNTAIN
BLUEBIRD

AMERICAN DIPPER

Golden Eagle

THE GOLDEN EAGLE, named for the golden feathers on its head and neck, is one of the largest and fiercest hunters in the North American bird world. The huge raptor—it has a seven-foot (2.1 m) wingspan—can soar effortlessly on rising air currents and spot a prey animal far below using its "eagle-eyed" vision.

SCIENTIFIC NAME: *Aquila chrysaetos*
LENGTH: 35 in (89 cm)
WINGSPAN: 84 in (213 cm)

With a dive that can reach 200 miles an hour (322 km/h), any rabbit or ground squirrel doesn't stand a chance. Native Americans regarded the eagle as a sacred bird with special powers. Because the Golden Eagle's feathers play an important role in the religious ceremonies of the Hopi nation, they have been given special permission from the United States government to remove hatched eagles from their nests and raise them in captivity.

VITAL STATISTICS

VOICE

Golden Eagles are not very vocal. Their call is a high, weak whistle most often heard during nesting season.

FOOD

Favorite foods are small mammals—mice and voles—and larger prey like jackrabbits, ground squirrels, prairie dogs, and marmots. They also eat snakes, lizards, birds, and large insects. Golden Eagles are capable of killing very large animals like foxes, young deer, lambs, and even coyotes, but that does not happen very often. Carrion is another important food source, and Golden Eagles often follow scavengers like crows and vultures to feeding sites.

HABITAT & RANGE

Golden Eagles live in many different places throughout the West from high in the mountains to deep in the desert. They are rare in the East. For nesting, a pair selects a high, secluded cliff or tall tree in which to build its large stick nest. Most eagles in the United States don't

DESPITE its broad wings, a Golden Eagle can quickly **change** direction and speed when it sees something edible down below.

A CLOSER LOOK

Adults are dark brown.

Adult

Pointed feathers on the head and neck are tinged with gold.

Unlike most other hawks and eagles, its legs are feathered, not bare.

Large eyes can spot prey from a great distance. A ridge of bone over the eyes protects them from the wind or a struggling animal.

Heavy hooked bill for tearing flesh and skin

Bright yellow toes with large, sharp talons are used for grabbing prey.

migrate; they live in the same area all year. Some that nest in the far north migrate south for the winter. Golden Eagles also live in Europe and Asia.

RANGE MAP KEY

- SUMMER (breeding)
- WINTER (nonbreeding)
- MIGRATION
- YEAR-ROUND

HUMAN IMPACT

Last century, Bald Eagles were dying out because they ate fish that were full of pesticides that washed into the water from farm fields. The poisonous chemicals caused Bald Eagles to lay eggs with very thin shells that broke when they were being incubated. Luckily, Golden Eagles don't eat much fish; they eat small, pesticide-free mammals and escaped the harm done to Bald Eagles. But other human activities threaten Golden Eagles. The construction of huge wind turbines in wilderness areas has led to collisions that have killed eagles; rural power poles often carry live wires that can electrocute them when the large birds' wings or feet make contact with two lines and form an electrical circuit; and even though there are laws protecting all eagles, some sheep ranchers still shoot and poison them, believing that the eagles are killing their lambs.

Steller's Jay

THE STELLER'S JAY is a large, turquoise, dark blue, and black bird with a shaggy-edged crest that lives in many western locations. These jays are especially common in mountain pine forests. Like other jays, Steller's are loud, bold, and curious, interacting with people in backyards, parks, and campgrounds. They fly on broad wings, interspersing flapping with gliding, and make a lot of noise with their harsh, scolding calls. In wilder places and especially when nesting they can be very shy. In the fall and winter, they form small flocks and cooperate with each other. A "sentry" bird will stand guard, alert for any danger, while the others in the flock forage quietly, knowing that their backs are covered.

SCIENTIFIC NAME: *Cyanocitta stelleri*
LENGTH: 11½ in (29 cm)
WINGSPAN: 19 in (48 cm)

VITAL STATISTICS

VOICE

Steller's Jays have a variety of calls that include a piercing *SHECK-SHECK-SHECK* and a harsh, *JEAAHHH*. Other sounds include a variety of rattles and whistles. Skillful mimics, Steller's Jays often imitate the sounds that other birds and animals make. The most common imitation is the screaming call of a Red-tailed Hawk, but they also mimic squirrel calls, barking dogs, and chickens.

FOOD

In the wild, Steller's Jays eat insects, small animals, seeds, berries, and nuts; and sometimes other birds' eggs and nestlings. They feed in trees and on the ground. In picnic areas and campgrounds they eat anything they can steal or convince people to offer to them. They are easily attracted to backyard bird feeders.

HABITAT & RANGE

Steller's Jays live in tall-timber country—usually evergreens or evergreens mixed with deciduous trees like oaks—from sea level to high in the mountains. Their nest is a cup of twigs and leaves with an inner lining of grass situated high in a tree on a horizontal limb. Though Steller's Jays do not usually migrate, they sometimes move to lower elevations in winter. These birds also live in Mexico and Central America.

STELLER'S JAYS can glide down from the treetops by simply opening and closing their **short wings.**

A CLOSER LOOK

Long blackish crest. The only other jay with a crest is the Blue Jay, which lives in the East.

Vivid blue wings with fine black barring

Long tail helps to maneuver when flying in tight spaces.

Most birds have blue lines on the head; birds from the southern Rockies have white lines.

Powerful bill handles varied foods, from acorns to lizards.

RANGE MAP KEY

WINTER (nonbreeding)   YEAR-ROUND

CACHING AND CASHING IN

Steller's Jays hide acorns and pine nuts to eat later when there is less food available (caching). They have excellent memories and can remember where hundreds of different food stashes are located. They also are sneak thieves. If one jay sees another taking a nut off to be stashed, it watches from a distance and, after the other bird leaves, moves in for the heist. These jays also know that "it takes a thief to know a thief." If a jay notices another jay watching, it waits until it's sure that the other bird is gone before it hides its prize nut.

American Dipper

AMERICAN DIPPERS are plump, gray birds about the size of a robin. Although they look drab and boring, they live one of the most unusual lives of any songbird. They are the only songbird in North America to swim and dive underwater to hunt for their food. In fact, dippers are very rarely found far from a fast-flowing stream. You might think that they are called dippers because they go for a "dip" in the water, but there's another reason. Dippers got their name from the up-and-down—or dipping—motion that they make. They do it constantly, but no one is sure why. Perhaps it is a visual signal to other dippers around noisy streams where even their loud calls might be drowned out.

SCIENTIFIC NAME: *Cinclus mexicanus*
LENGTH: 7½ in (19 cm)
WINGSPAN: 11 in (28 cm)

VOICE

It takes a loud voice to be heard over the sounds of a roaring stream, and the dipper's song is loud and musical. Most importantly, it is pitched higher than the sounds made by rushing water, so it can be easily heard above the noise of the stream. Its short call is a loud, buzzy *dzeet*.

FOOD

Aquatic insects and their larvae, small fish, and fish eggs are all on the menu. Using its unique ability to swim underwater and to dive up to six feet (1.8 m) below the surface, the dipper can take advantage of a food source unavailable to other small birds. On the stream bottom, its strong claws hold it in place and it uses its bill to probe under rocks. It uses its wings underwater to get from place to place and to chase after small fish.

HABITAT & RANGE

Most dippers live along fast-flowing, unpolluted mountain streams in western North America. Some dippers live along coastal streams from northern California to

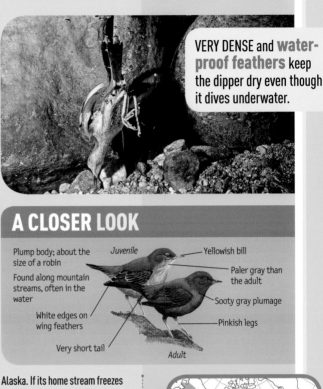

VERY DENSE and **water-proof feathers** keep the dipper dry even though it dives underwater.

A CLOSER LOOK

Plump body; about the size of a robin

Found along mountain streams, often in the water

White edges on wing feathers

Very short tail

Juvenile

Yellowish bill

Paler gray than the adult

Sooty gray plumage

Pinkish legs

Adult

Alaska. If its home stream freezes over in winter, the dipper moves to a lower elevation or closer to the coast. American Dippers also live in mountainous areas of Mexico and Central America.

RANGE MAP KEY

WINTER (nonbreeding)

YEAR-ROUND

A HOME BEHIND A WATERFALL

To us, the space behind a waterfall looks like a beautiful setting, but the dipper has good reasons to build a nest there: It provides a safe shelter for baby dippers, protection from predators, and waterfalls are close to streams full of food. Sometimes, nests are located in a streamside crevice, but small waterfalls seem to be preferred. The parents build a snug, soccer-ball-size nest out of moss and leaves, complete with an entrance facing the water and an overhang to keep out any water spray. Four or five young dippers hatch about two weeks after the eggs are laid.

Mountain Bluebird

A SMALL MEMBER of the thrush family, the Mountain Bluebird nests high in the mountains and also lives in open areas and ranchland in the American West. Males are a dreamy sky-blue color, and the female is cloaked in soft brownish gray. When spring arrives, the male claims a nest hole and defends it from rival males. Suitable nest holes can be hard to find, and he needs a good location in order to attract a female to mate with. Inside the cavity, the female does most of the nest building, weaving together a cozy nest cup of weed stems, grass, and pine needles and lining it with feathers, moss, and hair. She lays five to six pale blue eggs and sits on them for about two weeks before they hatch.

SCIENTIFIC NAME: *Sialia currucoides*
LENGTH: 7¼ in (18 cm)
WINGSPAN: 14 in (36 cm)

VITAL STATISTICS

VOICE

The Mountain Bluebird's song is a series of short, warbled notes, *tru-lee tru-lee*, and its call is a thin, nasal-sounding *few*.

FOOD

Bluebirds are insect eaters. In the summer, their diet consists mostly of beetles, grasshoppers, crickets, caterpillars, ants, and bees. Their usual hunting method is dropping down from a perch to catch an insect on the ground, but they also catch bugs on the fly and hover over grasslands searching for prey. During the winter, they supplement their insect diet with fruit and berries.

HABITAT & RANGE

During summer, Mountain Bluebirds prefer open country with some trees, usually at high elevations—from 5,000 up to 12,000 feet (1,524 to 3,658 m). They nest in old woodpecker holes and other cavities and also birdhouses. For the winter, Mountain Bluebirds move to lower elevations. Small flocks congregate to forage in open woodlands or over grasslands and alfalfa fields. Seeing a winter flock of these

THE female Mountain Bluebird is actually brownish **gray** with just a hint of blue on her wings and tail.

A CLOSER LOOK

Very long wings allow it to hover briefly while searching for insects on the ground.

Powder-blue belly and slightly darker blue above

Female

Male

Fine-tipped bill is perfect for catching small insects.

sky-blue birds hovering over a field is a very special experience. Birds nesting in Canada and Alaska migrate south in the fall. In the Rockies, birds move to lower elevations in fall, and sometimes they stray to the East Coast in winter.

RANGE MAP KEY

- ■ SUMMER (breeding)
- ■ WINTER (nonbreeding)
- □ MIGRATION
- ■ YEAR-ROUND

I'M OUTTA HERE

Young bluebirds—and many other kinds of birds—are often anxious to leave their nest or birdhouse, even before they can fly. Maybe it gets cramped in there or maybe they just know that it's safer outside. Snakes and raccoons often try to raid bluebird nests. The young birds' spotted plumage is good camouflage if they have to hop around on the ground for a few days before getting airborne. They also have very loud begging calls, so their parents will know where they are and feed them.

Western Tanager

VIVIDLY BEAUTIFUL, the male Western Tanager has a black-and-yellow body and a bright red head. They show quite a bit of variation in the amount of red coloring on the head due to their unique way of obtaining pigment—they eat it! Western Tanagers do not manufacture the red pigment the way other tanagers do; it comes from insects the birds eat during breeding season. Imagine if you ate a diet of cherry Popsicles and your hair turned red.

During migration and in winter, males mostly eat fruit and lose the red color of their heads. Brightly colored Western Tanagers can be surprisingly difficult to find when they are feeding on insects high up in the trees. But seeing your first one through binoculars is something you'll never forget.

SCIENTIFIC NAME: *Piranga ludoviciana*
LENGTH: 7¼ in (18 cm)
WINGSPAN: 11½ in (29 cm)

VOICE

Western Tanagers have been described as having a short, burry song that sounds "like a robin with a sore throat." Their call is a piercing *pit-er-ICK!*

FOOD

Caterpillars, bees, wasps, beetles, grasshoppers, termites, and cicadas are just some of the insects that make up the Western Tanager's diet. They often feed in the treetops, moving slowly from branch to branch, picking insects off of the vegetation. Flying insects are sometimes caught on the wing, and flowers are searched for insects that might be hidden inside a blossom, attracted to the nectar. Berries and some cultivated fruit are also eaten, especially in winter.

HABITAT & RANGE

Western Tanagers breed in the high mountains in evergreen or aspen forests, sometimes in the far north. During migration, they occur in every habitat in the West, even the desert. A few Western Tanagers spend the winter in California eucalyptus groves, but most fly south to their winter homes in Mexico and Central America.

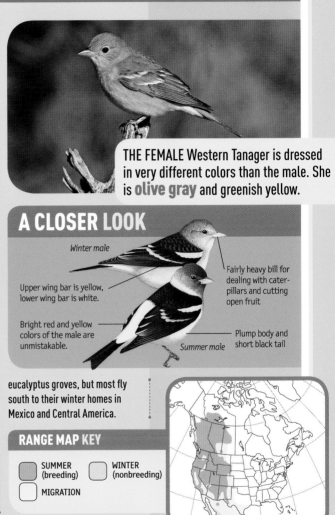

THE FEMALE Western Tanager is dressed in very different colors than the male. She is **olive gray** and greenish yellow.

A CLOSER LOOK

Winter male

Summer male

Upper wing bar is yellow, lower wing bar is white.

Bright red and yellow colors of the male are unmistakable.

Fairly heavy bill for dealing with caterpillars and cutting open fruit

Plump body and short black tail

RANGE MAP KEY

SUMMER (breeding)

WINTER (nonbreeding)

MIGRATION

GROWING UP FAST ... REALLY FAST

There's nothing unusual about the way baby Western Tanagers grow up; in fact, many songbirds have very similar life histories. After the female lays her three to five eggs, she sits on them (incubates them) for about 13 days until they hatch. Both parents feed the nestlings a diet of insects. The nestlings grow their first coat of feathers in about 10 to 14 days. At this point they can fly, and leave the nest, never to return. (Nests are actually dangerous places because of the predators that eat eggs and baby birds, so leaving fast is a good thing.) The parents feed the young birds and shepherd them around the neighborhood for about two more weeks. That's it, from hatching to college graduate in about a month!

Mini-Profiles

WESTERN MOUNTAINS

The famous national parks in the Rockies are great places to look for birds that love forests of evergreens and aspens. Next time you're at a park or anywhere else outdoors in the Rockies area, keep your eyes peeled for these birds.

WHITE-TAILED PTARMIGAN

SCIENTIFIC NAME: *Lagopus leucura*
LENGTH: 12½ in (32 cm)
WINGSPAN: 22 in (56 cm)

White-tailed Ptarmigans (TAR-meh-gehns, with a silent "p") are tame, chickenlike birds that like cold weather. During the summer, if the temperature gets above 70°F (21°C) they go looking for a snowbank to cool off in. These small members of the grouse family are masters of camouflage. In winter their plumage is snowy white, and in summer they grow a whole new set of mottled brown feathers that make them look just like rocks. Adults are vegetarians, feeding on the buds and leaves of low-growing alpine plants. Very young chicks consume a protein-rich diet of insects.

WHITE-THROATED SWIFT

SCIENTIFIC NAME: *Aeronautes saxatalis*
LENGTH: 6½ in (17 cm)
WINGSPAN: 15 in (38 cm)

The White-throated Swift is one of the fastest flying birds in North America and spends the entire day in the air pursuing flying insects. Its plumage is black with a white throat and a white line down the belly. Flying birds have thin, swept-back wings and hold their long tails in a point. In the Rockies, White-throated Swifts cruise high above steep-walled canyons and river gorges. In southern and central California, they fly above coastal cliffs and are seen soaring over cities. Nests are located in cliff crevices and holes in canyon walls. The saucer-like nest is made of weed stems, grass, and feathers, all glued together with the swift's sticky saliva.

BROAD-TAILED HUMMINGBIRD

SCIENTIFIC NAME: *Selasphorus platycercus*
LENGTH: 4 in (10 cm)
WINGSPAN: 5¼ in (13 cm)

Broad-tailed Hummingbirds nest at high elevations in the central and southern Rocky Mountains, where they feed on the nectar of abundant wildflowers and swarm around hummingbird feeders when they can. The male has a rose red throat; the female's throat is white with green spots. This tiny bird is well adapted to survival in the mountains, where nights can be cold even during the summer. It can enter a body state called torpor, lowering its body temperature and slowing its heart rate to save enough calories to survive the night. The female does all of the nest building, incubates the eggs, and feeds the two nestlings.

CLARK'S NUTCRACKER

SCIENTIFIC NAME: *Nucifraga columbiana*
LENGTH: 12 in (31 cm)
WINGSPAN: 24 in (61 cm)

The Clark's Nutcracker is a crowlike, mountain bird with a gray body, black wings and tail, and a patch of white under the tail. This noisy bird is often heard before it is seen. Its call is loud and drawn out—a harsh, grating *KRA-A-A*. Although nutcrackers live high in the mountains and far from people, these bold birds are often encountered at scenic overlooks along mountain roads and in picnic areas and campgrounds looking for a handout. They normally depend on pine nuts (conifer seeds) for their main food. During summer and fall, the birds harvest thousands of seeds and store them in hidden caches. Remarkably, the birds remember where almost all of the hiding places are.

VIOLET-GREEN SWALLOW

SCIENTIFIC NAME: *Tachycineta thalassina*
LENGTH: 5¼ in (13 cm)
WINGSPAN: 13½ in (34 cm)

The colorful Violet-green Swallow has a moss green back and head, and a rump tinged with glossy violet. Its pure white underparts and face sometimes cause it to be confused with the White-throated Swift (see opposite page), but it has broader wings and flies with slower, fluttery wing beats. Like other swallows, the Violet-green feeds on flying insects. During the summer months, it is common to see small flocks flying over pine forests in the Rocky Mountains and other western locations all the way to Alaska. They nest in tree cavities, holes in cliffs, and even in birdhouses. As summer draws to a close, Violet-green Swallows migrate to their winter home in Mexico.

MOUNTAIN CHICKADEE

SCIENTIFIC NAME: *Poecile gambeli*
LENGTH: 8½ in (22 cm)
WINGSPAN: 15 in (38 cm)

The white stripe over the eye of the Mountain Chickadee separates it from the five other kinds of chickadees in North America. It is one of the most common birds in western mountain forests. Like other chickadees, its *chick-a-dee-dee* call sounds like its name. In typical chickadee fashion, it is always busy. Hunting for pine seeds and then hiding those seeds for a future meal (known as "caching," pronounced cash-ing) takes a lot of time. Small social groups of Mountain Chickadees defend a territory from other chickadee groups that might steal their hidden seeds.

SNOWY OWL

Rock Star

Birds

Rock Star Birds of North America

ATLANTIC PUFFIN

SCIENTIFIC NAME: *Fratercula arctica*
LENGTH: 12½ in (32 cm)
WINGSPAN: 21 in (53 cm)

Puffins look like penguins wearing clown masks, with their black-and-white bodies and huge, multicolored bills. They aren't penguins; they are members of a family of seabirds called auks. Unlike penguins, the puffin's wings allow it to fly in the air as well as under the water. (Penguins only use their wings under water. They can't fly.) Atlantic Puffins breed on rocky islands off the coast of Maine and farther north, and spend winters at sea in the North Atlantic. The puffin has the ability to hold up to a dozen slippery, eel-like fish in its bill at one time.

TRUMPETER SWAN

SCIENTIFIC NAME: *Cygnus buccinator*
LENGTH: 60 in (152 cm)
WINGSPAN: 80 in (203 cm)

The big, noisy Trumpeter Swan flaps its long wings up to Alaska each spring, to nest on the marshy edges of ponds and lakes. Winters are spent not very far south, on ice-free lakes and rivers in the northern U.S. and western Canada. Swans form pair bonds when they are three or four years old and stay together throughout the year, migrating in the same flock, often for a lifetime, which can last more than 20 years. Trumpeter Swans were hunted almost to extinction by the late 1800s, because their long flight feathers made the finest quill pens.

ROSEATE SPOONBILL

SCIENTIFIC NAME: *Platalea ajaja*
LENGTH: 32 in (81 cm)
WINGSPAN: 50 in (127 cm)

Because of the Roseate Spoonbill's bright pink color, first-time observers in southern Florida and along the Gulf Coast often think they're seeing a flamingo. Take a closer look and you'll see the differences. The spoonbill has a wide flattened bill, bald greenish head, and shorter legs. To feed, the spoonbill swings its spoon-shaped bill from side to side until it feels a small fish or other tasty morsel. Like other large waterbirds, the spoonbill was hunted almost to extinction during the late 19th century for its beautiful feathers, which were used to decorate women's hats.

SNOWY OWL

SCIENTIFIC NAME: *Bubo scandiacus*
LENGTH: 23 in (58 cm)
WINGSPAN: 52 in (132 cm)

Known as the "ghost hunter of the North," a Snowy Owl played a prominent role in the Harry Potter series as Hedwig, Harry's messenger owl. Some Snowy Owls live in their Arctic tundra home all year long, while others migrate south in winter to southern Canada, New England, New York, and the northern plains states. In some years they can be found in the Midwest and Pacific Northwest. Unlike most owls, Snowy Owls hunt during the day, which can last 24 hours during the Arctic summer. Their main food is a small rodent called a lemming, and a single bird can eat more than 1,600 lemmings in a year.

ELEGANT TROGON

SCIENTIFIC NAME: *Trogon elegans*
LENGTH: 12½ in (32 cm)
WINGSPAN: 16 in (41 cm)

The Elegant Trogon is a large, tropical forest bird with beautiful colors and a long tail. The male has a bright red belly, a glittering green head and back, and an iridescent, copper-colored tail. The female has the same elegant shape and copper-colored tail, but with less vivid colors on her body. In the U.S., the Elegant Trogon lives only in mountain canyons in Arizona, close to the border with Mexico. Every year an estimated 25,000 people visit the South Fork of Cave Creek in Arizona's Chiricahua Mountains to try to see it.

PAINTED BUNTING

SCIENTIFIC NAME: *Passerina ciris*
LENGTH: 5½ in (14 cm)
WINGSPAN: 8¾ in (22 cm)

The old southern name for Painted Bunting is "Nonpareil." It comes from the French language and means "having no equal," which is a perfect description of the incredible colors of the adult male Painted Bunting. The female's plumage is a subtle mix of green and pale yellow—good camouflage that keeps her safe when nesting. Painted Buntings live in lowland areas of the southeastern U.S.

191

HARPY EAGLE

SCIENTIFIC NAME: *Harpia harpyja*
LENGTH: 42 in (107 cm)
WINGSPAN: 80 in (203 cm)

The Harpy Eagle lives in the Neotropical rain forest and is the largest and most powerful eagle in the world. It flies through the forest—expertly dodging tree trunks and branches—on massive wings, hunting medium-size mammals. Its prey is snatched up by its powerful legs and feet and carried off held in its eight massive talons. Monkeys and anteaters are frequent prey, but its favorite food is the tree-dwelling sloth, which can weigh up to 20 pounds (9.1 kg), about the same weight as the Harpy Eagle itself.

EMPEROR PENGUIN

SCIENTIFIC NAME: *Aptenodytes forsteri*
LENGTH: 38 in (97 cm)
WEIGHT: up to 100 lbs (45 kg)—flightless

All of the world's 17 species of penguin live in the Southern Hemisphere. The Emperor Penguin, which lives in Antarctica, is the biggest. All penguins are flightless, but Emperor Penguins walk as much as 125 miles (201 km) inland from their fishing grounds to gather in huge breeding colonies every year. Each pair lays a single egg. The male incubates it—on his feet!—for two months in winter weather that can go down to 60° below zero F (-51°C) and has nothing to eat for the entire time. The female walks back to the coast to feed and trades off parenting duties with the male after the egg has hatched.

KEEL-BILLED TOUCAN

SCIENTIFIC NAME: *Ramphastos sulfuratus*
LENGTH: 28 in (71 cm)
WINGSPAN: 50 in (127 cm)

A huge colorful bill makes the toucan easy to identify. Toucans live in the New World tropics, where their huge bills allow them to reach fruits at the end of branches too skinny to support their weight. These bills are used to explore tree cavities looking for frogs, lizards, and other things to eat. The bill looks heavy, but is actually very light and strong, and is covered with a layer of keratin, the very same biological material that your fingernails are made of. Keel-billed Toucans live in lowland forests from southern Mexico to Venezuela.

OSTRICH

SCIENTIFIC NAME: *Struthio camelus*
LENGTH: 96 in (244 cm)
WEIGHT: up to 320 lbs (145 kg)—flightless

The Ostrich, the world's largest living bird, is taller than a human adult and lives in Africa. It can't fly, but that's not a problem, as it can run at more than 40 miles an hour (64 km/h) across open ground. Contrary to popular belief, the Ostrich does not bury its head in the sand, but often lies down with its head on the ground when hiding from a predator, such as a lion. If it's threatened, it kicks out with its powerful legs and fistlike feet, a deadly combination.

RESPLENDENT QUETZAL

SCIENTIFIC NAME: *Pharomachrus mocinno*
LENGTH: 14 in (36 cm), plus 24 in (61 cm) for male's plumes
WINGSPAN: 22 in (55 cm)

The Resplendent Quetzal (pronounced KET-zawl) is the most beautiful bird in the Western Hemisphere. The male has long, trailing plumes up to two feet (0.6 m) long, which twist and dance when he flies, giving him a magical quality in the air. Quetzals primarily eat fruit—wild avocado is a favorite—which is swallowed whole. Later on, the seed is regurgitated (spit up) in a different place and some-time sprouts, thus producing a new tree and eventually more food for the quetzal.

WANDERING ALBATROSS

SCIENTIFIC NAME: *Diomedea exulans*
LENGTH: 50 in (127 cm)
WINGSPAN: 132 in (335 cm)

Superstitious sailors believe that seeing an albatross is good luck, but killing one will curse their ship and everyone aboard. The Wandering Albatross is an awe-inspiring bird. It has the longest wingspan—almost 11 feet (3.4 m) from tip to tip—and is the most powerful flyer of all the world's seabirds. Some individuals are known to fly 100,000 miles (161,000 km) a year without ever touching land—that's almost halfway to the moon! Young birds spend up to 10 years at sea, until they are mature enough to mate and raise a family—one chick every other year—on remote ocean islands.

Birds Behaving Badly
North America

NORTHERN FULMAR

SCIENTIFIC NAME: *Fulmarus glacialis*
LENGTH: 19 in (48 cm)
WINGSPAN: 42 in (107 cm)

Most birds defend themselves with their beaks and sharp claws or simply by flying away. The fulmar (which means "foul gull") has a different and unexpected weapon—stinky stomach oil that can be accurately aimed at an intruder up to six feet (1.8 m) away. That's gross but also highly effective. The fulmar's barf bomb of oil can sometimes even kill. Feathers soaked with stomach oil can render an attacker unable to fly, swim, or stay warm. Fulmars are gull-size birds that spend most of the year at sea.

PARASITIC JAEGER

SCIENTIFIC NAME: *Stercorarius parasiticus*
LENGTH: 19 in (48 cm)
WEIGHT: 42 in (107 cm)

Jaeger (pronounced yeah-gur) is German for "hunter," but the jaeger is better described as a pirate. "Parasitic" means living at the expense of another species and sometimes causing its death. What does the Parasitic Jaeger do to be called a death-dealing pirate? In summer it nests on the Arctic tundra and kills birds and mammals and steals eggs to feed itself and its chicks. It's not much different than what a hawk or falcon does. The rest of the year is spent living at sea ... as a pirate. A jaeger can fly fast and make amazingly quick turns. It uses these skills to chase after a smaller seabird to steal its meal. The other bird gets so tired from trying to escape that it drops the fish it is carrying or throws up its stomach contents. Then the pirate-hunter stops chasing and has its dinner.

NORTHERN GANNET

SCIENTIFIC NAME: *Morus bassanus*
LENGTH: 37 in (94 cm)
WINGSPAN: 72 in (180 cm)

Gannets are huge birds that live at sea for most of the year. During the summer months they nest in huge colonies on rocky cliffs, but real estate is very limited and the birds are tightly packed together. Birds are constantly squawking and pecking at their neighbors with their long and very pointed bills. Each nest is located precisely as far from the next nest as a gannet can reach with a violent thrust of its bill. Inches of territory are hotly defended and birds can often end up bloodied.

MISSISSIPPI KITE

SCIENTIFIC NAME: *Ictinia mississippiensis*
LENGTH: 14½ in (37 cm)
WEIGHT: 35 in (89 cm)

The Mississippi Kite (a kind of hawk) nests in tall trees bordering open areas in the southern U.S. Golf courses are a favorite place to nest. So what's the problem? The problem is that the Mississippi Kites don't like golfers getting near their nests. They dive at intruders trying to get them to leave. When they have young in their nests, they go to war. Get too close and you risk sharp talons aimed at your head. Makes for an exciting game of golf! Despite the occasional attack, most people enjoy having these graceful birds living near them.

NORTHERN SHRIKE

SCIENTIFIC NAME: *Lanius excubitor*
LENGTH: 10 in (25 cm)
WINGSPAN: 14½ in (37 cm)

Although scientists classify the Northern Shrike as a songbird, the translation of its scientific name is "butcher watchman." Although smaller than a robin, it strikes fear in birds larger than itself, as well as in mice and voles. It is usually seen scanning for prey from a perch in a tall tree. When it spies a victim, it attacks it on or near the ground and kills it with a swift bite to the neck from its hooked bill. The dead animal is carried to a "butchering" location—usually a bush with large thorns or a barbed wire fence—where it is pinned. Northern Shrikes nest in the Arctic and spends the winter in southern Canada and the northern U.S.

BROWN-HEADED COWBIRD

SCIENTIFIC NAME: *Molothrus ater*
LENGTH: 7½ in (19 cm)
WINGSPAN: 12 in (30 cm)

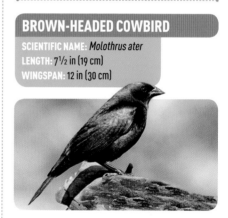

Brown-headed Cowbirds get other birds to raise their young. The female sneaks around until she finds the nest of another bird (the host) and then lays one or two eggs there. Sometimes she pushes the host's eggs out of the nest before disappearing. When the cowbird eggs hatch, the host bird does all the work of feeding and caring for the babies. Animals that live at the expense of other animals are called parasites—fleas and ticks are good examples. The word "parasite" comes from an ancient Greek word that translates as "eating at another's table." That's what the baby cowbird is doing.

How to Build a Bird Feeder

SODA BOTTLE BIRD FEEDER

Feeding birds is fun. If you hang a bird feeder near a window, you can look out and see an amazing parade of beautiful birds. It's easy to make your own bird feeder, and it doesn't cost a lot. The birds will like it just as much as an expensive store-bought one. During the winter months when food is scarce, the seed you provide may help the birds survive. When it's warm out, the birds can find their own food, but you can still feed them if you want to. You can find birdseed for your feeder at most grocery, hardware, and pet stores. Mixed birdseed will do the job and is not expensive, but the best seed for wild birds is black-oil sunflower seed, which doesn't cost much more.

MATERIALS YOU WILL NEED

- 1 two-liter plastic soda (or water) bottle
- Ruler
- Marker
- Utility knife
- 2 wooden spoons
- 1 small screw eye
- Twine for hanging
- Birdseed
- Funnel

1 Remove the outside wrapper from the plastic bottle, rinse the bottle well, and turn it upside down to dry.

---

2 With a ruler, measure 2 inches up from the bottom and use the marker to draw a ½-inch "X" to mark the spot. Then, turn the bottle 90 degrees and measure 5 inches up

from the bottom and draw another ½-inch "X" to mark the spot. Then draw a 1-inch-wide circle opposite both of the X-marks, as shown.

3 This next step is a parent or guardian's job. Ask an adult to use the utility knife to slit the two X-marks and cut out the 1-inch circles.

4 Insert a wooden spoon handle through each of the cutout circles and then push handles through the X-mark. The wooden spoons will act as a perch and also catch seed that falls out.

5 The first part of this step is also a parent or guardian's job. Ask an adult to remove the cap and use the utility knife to poke a small hole in the top of it. Then you can take the screw eye and twist it into the center of the top. Next, attach a piece of twine to the screw eye and tie it tightly in a knot. The length of the twine will depend on the height of the branch or bird feeder hanger you want to hang the feeder from. You may want to take the twine and hang it from the branch or hanger to see how far down you would like your feeder to be.

6 Now you're almost done. Fill your feeder with birdseed—use the funnel to pour the seed into the small opening. Before you put the cap back on, hang it from the tree first. The easiest way to hang the bird feeder is to use a slipknot. Then screw your bird feeder on. You may need an adult to help you. Now you're done! Sit back, relax, and enjoy all of the wonderful birds you will see!

NOTE: Location is important! Hang your feeder far enough away from bushes so that a hungry cat can't reach it in a single pounce. If you want to watch the feeder from inside, hang it near a window, but make sure it is no more than a foot away from the glass. If it's farther away, a bird that is scared off can fly full speed into the window glass and hurt itself.

How to Make a Birdbath

Birds don't need anything fancy or compli-cated, just a shallow pool of water to drink and splash in—they'll use a puddle in the road, if they find one.

A simple birdbath can be set up using three flowerpots and a plant saucer—the kind that goes under a potted plant. It can be made of clay or plastic, depending on what you prefer.

MATERIALS YOU WILL NEED

• **Three clay flowerpots,** with diameters that differ by two inches (one 12", one 14", and one 16", for example)

• **One clay plant saucer.** Make sure the saucer is at least a few inches wider than the bottom of your smallest flowerpot so it is big enough for the birds to enjoy!

• **Water-based clear gloss paint sealant** (this item should be used only by a grown-up).

• **Acrylic paints in assorted colors.** Make sure the paints you buy are weather resis-tant. Patio paint is a good option.

• **Paintbrushes**

• **Super glue** (this item should be used only by a grown-up).

MAKING YOUR BIRDBATH

1. Stack your flowerpots upside down with the largest one on the bottom, the medium size one in the middle, and the smallest one on top.

2. Mark dots around the rim of each flowerpot with a pencil so you know which parts of the pots will be covered.

3. Ask an adult to seal the inside of each pot and the saucer with two or three coats of the water-based sealant. Allow the sealant to dry. (Placing the items in the sun will help them to dry quickly.) Ask a grown-up to make sure the pots and saucer are completely dry.

4. Once the pots are completely dry, start painting! Use your imagination and be creative!

5. Once you are done painting, let your bird-bath dry completely.

ASSEMBLING YOUR BIRDBATH

1. The first step must be done by a grown-up: Use the super glue to glue the bottom of the plant saucer to the bottom of the smallest flowerpot.

2. Let the saucer and small flowerpot dry completely. It is best if you allow it to dry overnight.

3. When the saucer and small pot are dry, choose a location for your birdbath and take all materials to that location to start putting your birdbath together.

4. Once you have the perfect location, turn the largest flowerpot upside down and place the medium-size flowerpot on top of it, upside down. Then place the small flowerpot, with saucer attached, on top of the medium pot, also upside down.

5. Your birdbath is now complete! All you have to do is add some water and enjoy the bird-watching!

Be sure to change the water every three or four days, and clean the birdbath, especially the saucer, weekly to prevent algae or bacteria from growing.

NOTE: Instead of clay pots, you can buy sturdy, weather-resistant plastic flowerpots and saucers. If you buy plastic, you may want to purchase them in different colors or with different patterns for variety. Then follow the instructions under "Assembling Your Birdbath."

How to Build a Bird Nest

Many bird species use the materials they find near their nesting areas to weave a shelter where they can lay their eggs, keep the eggs safe and warm until they hatch, and then protect and feed their nestlings until they can fly on their own two wings. If you have ever found a bird's nest and looked at it closely, you were probably amazed at the way the bird wove together natural materials to form a cozy cup or a basket of sticks. Now you can build one of your own!

MATERIALS YOU WILL NEED

- **A plastic tarp** or large plastic bag
- **Scissors**
- **A paper bag**
- **Colored construction paper**
- **A cereal bowl** for the nest mold
- **Plastic wrap**
- **School glue**
- **2 small paper cups**
- **Water**
- **A bowl** for the glue and water mixture
- **A plastic spoon**
- **Feathers and moss** (You can find these at a craft store.)

PUTTING YOUR BIRD NEST TOGETHER

1. Set up a plastic tarp or large plastic bag to use as your surface for making the nest. Place all materials on the tarp or bag.

2. Cut the paper bag and the colored construction paper into strips about ½-inch thick and put them aside.

3. Cover the outside of your cereal bowl with plastic wrap (this is to ensure the nest won't stick to the bowl when it's dry).

4. Pour about 3 ounces of glue into one of the small paper cups and 3 ounces of water into the other. Then pour both into your mixing bowl.

5. Use the plastic spoon to stir the glue and water together until they are completely mixed.

6. Dip your strips of paper one by one into the mixture and start placing them on top of the cereal bowl.

7. Keep layering until the entire bowl is covered, then repeat until you have covered the bowl in two or three layers of paper. Use as many colors as you like and make sure to layer the paper at different angles.

8. Every now and then, gently smooth the strips down.

9. When you're done, allow this to dry for about 24 hours.

10. When the nest is completely dry, carefully remove the nest from the plastic surface, and then carefully remove the plastic wrap from the nest. You should now have a lovely bird nest!

11. Carefully glue your feathers and moss inside the nest. (Birds often use different materials to line their nest to keep eggs and babies warm.)

12. Your bird nest is now complete!

How to Draw a Bird

Drawing birds can be easy and fun, once you learn a few basic steps. Looking closely at a bird in order to draw it is a great way to learn more about it. You can also look at photos or paintings of birds. Start with blank white paper, a sharp #2 pencil, and a good eraser. You can add color later with colored pencils or watercolors. Don't press too hard with your pencil at the start. It'll be easier to erase when you want to.

1. DRAW THE BASIC SHAPES
Start with two ovals—a large one for the body and a smaller one for the head. Some birds have large heads and others have small ones, compared to the size of their bodies. At the rear end, a wedge shape connects the tail to the body. How long is the tail, compared to the body? Add lines close together under the body oval if you want the bird's feet to have a branch to perch on.

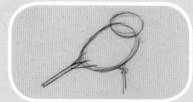

2. IMPROVE THE SHAPE OF THE BIRD
Add slightly curved lines at the throat and the back of the head to connect the head and body. Erase the inside lines where the two circles meet; they are no longer needed. Add a shape for the bill and a small circle for the eye—the eyes usually are close to the bill, not in the center of the head. Draw a slightly stretched-out oval for the folded wing. Draw the legs where they come out of the body toward the branch (or the ground, if you are

drawing a standing bird instead of a perching one). Erase any lines that you no longer need, and darken the ones that you want to keep.

3. ADD DETAILS
Keep working on the shapes, and start to add feather details in the wings and tail. When working on the wings, pay attention to how the feathers overlap. Add details to the bill and draw the feet gripping the branch (or on the ground).

4. ADD PATTERNS AND SHADING
When the shape and feather outlines of the bird are done, you can draw in the light and dark patterns of the bird. Use light pressure with the side of the pencil's tip for lighter areas and heavier pressure with the pencil tip for darker areas or stripes. If the bird is colorful, use your colored pencils or watercolors.

5. IDENTIFY THE BIRD
Write the name of the bird on your drawing, and the date that you drew it. It's lots of fun to go back later to see the drawings you've done in the past!

Glossary

bill: The tough, outside covering of a bird's jaw. Bills (or beaks) come in all shapes and sizes, usually adapted to what the bird feeds on. Bills are made of the same material as a person's fingernails.

call: Bird sounds that are generally shorter than songs and made by both males and females. Calls convey a specific message. Unlike songs, calls are not learned; each bird is born knowing the unique calls that its species makes. (*See* song.)

egg: The way all birds reproduce. The tiny embryo is nourished by the attached food supply (the yolk) and surrounded by a cushion of watery gel (the white); the whole thing is enclosed in a hard calcium case (the eggshell).

extinct bird: A species of bird that no longer exists anywhere in the world

feather: Feathers are unique to birds. Different types of feathers serve different functions, from strong wing feathers for flight to soft, downy feathers for insulation.

flock: A group of birds; can be of all the same species, or a mixed flock made up of different species.

immature: Not fully adult. For some birds, such as the Bald Eagle, it takes four to five years to reach adult plumage. Some immature birds are capable of breeding.

incubation: Maintaining the eggs at an even temperature, usually in a nest, until they hatch

juvenile: A young bird wearing its first coat of feathers (not the down it hatches in).

A bird grows to its full adult size within the first year of life. Although full-grown, a juvenile can still look different from an adult because its feathers have different colors or patterns. (*See* immature.)

migration: The regular movement of birds to and from an area. In North America, *spring migration* is usually the northbound movement of birds to their breeding grounds; *fall migration* is the southbound movement of birds to the area where they spend the winter. Many species do not migrate.

molt: The replacement of old feathers with new ones. Most species replace all of their feathers once a year, but they do it slowly over a period of weeks or months.

plumage: Term for all the feathers that cover a bird's body

preening: Feather maintenance behavior, in which a bird grasps a feather near its base, then nibbles along the shaft towards the tip. This action cleans and smooths the feather.

roost: To sleep, or the place where a bird sleeps

song: A pattern of notes usually sung by a male bird (sometimes a female) to attract a mate or defend a territory. Most young birds learn their song by copying an adult. (*See* call.)

songbird: A type of bird with a complex voice box that can sing more complex songs than other birds

wing bars: One or two colored bars (often white) that run across a bird's wing

Index

Find Out More

To learn more about birds and stay connected to young birders around the country, check out these books, movies, and websites.

BOOKS
Hiaasen, Carl. *Hoot.* Yearling, 2005

Hoose, Phillip. *Moonbird: A Year on the Wind With the Great Survivor B95.* Farrar, Straus, and Giroux, 2012

Koch, Maryjo. *Bird Egg Feather Nest.* Smithmark, 1999

MOVIES AND DVDS
BBC Video. *The Life of Birds* (NR documentary series)

Questar. *Hummingbirds: Magic in the Air* (NR documentary)

Sony Pictures. *Winged Migration* (rated G)

Warner Brothers. *March of the Penguins* (rated G)

WEBSITES
All About Birds (The Cornell Lab of Ornithology): www.allaboutbirds.org

Backyard Birding (National Geographic): www.nationalgeographic.com/animals/birds

Just for Kids (National Audubon Society): www.audubon.org/educate/kids

KidWings: www.kidwings.com

Photo Credits

Abbreviations: GI = Getty Images; NGYS = National Geographic Your Shot; SS = Shutterstock

FRONT COVER AND SPINE: All Canada Photos/GI; (hummingbird), Chesapeake Images/SS; (birdhouse), Galchenkova Ludmila/SS; (eggs in nest) D&D Photos/SS; (bald eagle), MCarter/SS; **BACK COVER:** (western tanager), Richard Cronberg/NGYS; (mute swan), Jim Nelson/NGYS; (binoculars), Andrei Shumskiy/SS; **INSIDE FRONT AND BACK COVER ILLUSTRATIONS:** Jonathan Alderfer; David Beadle; Peter Burke; Marc R. Hanson; Cynthia J. House; H. Jon Janosik; Donald L. Malick; John P. O'Neill; Kent Pendleton; Diane Pierce; John C. Pitcher; H. Douglas Pratt; David Quinn; N. John Schmitt; Thomas R. Schultz; Daniel S. Smith; **FRONT MATTER:** 2-3, Delpho/ARCO/naturepl.com; 4, Thy Bun/NGYS; 5 (LE), George Quiroga/NGYS; 5 (RT), Geoff Powell/NGYS; 6, Bill Dodsworth/NGYS; 8-9, Akihiro Asami/NGYS; 12, Rohan Kulkarni/NGYS; 13 (LE), All Canada Photos/GI; 13 (RT), Stuart Clarke/NGYS; 14, John Warburton-Lee/AWL Images RM/GI; 15 (LE), James Cumming/NGYS; 15 (RT), Pam Morris/NGYS; **EASTERN BACKYARD:** 16-17, Robin Loznak/NGYS; 18 (LE), Steven Russell Smith Photos/SS; 18 (RT), Arindam Bhattacharya/NGYS; 19 (UP), Joey Bamburg/NGYS; 19 (CTR), Jim Ridley/NGYS; 19 (LO), L F File/SS; 20, Joey Bamburg/NGYS; 21 (UP), Michelle Earle/NGYS; 21 (CTR), N John Schmitt; 21 (LO), Bill Telzerow/NGYS; 22, Jim Ridley/NGYS; 23 (UP), Sharon and Mike Tobin/NGYS; 23 (CTR), H. Douglas Pratt; 23 (LO), Thomas Voyd/NGYS; 24, Brian Lasenby/SS/SS; 25 (UP), Mircea C/SS; 25 (CTR), Michael O'Brien; 25 (LO), papermeadow/iStockphoto/GI; 26, Nuwan Ganganath/NGYS; 27 (UP), Julia Martin/NGYS; 27 (CTR), H. Douglas Pratt; 27 (LO), Roman Zhitenev/NGYS; 28, Jim Ridley/NGYS; 29 (UP), Pam Morris/NGYS; 29 (CTR), Diane Pierce; 29 (LO), William Mullins/Alamy; 30 (UP), Steve Brigman/SS; 30 (CTR), Jim Nelson/NGYS; 30 (LO), p.schwarz/SS; 31 (UP), Dawn J Benko/SS; 31 (CTR), Alex Snyder;31 (LO), Gerald Marella/SS; 32 (UP), Steve Byland/SS; 32 (CTR), Tim Zurowski/SS; 32 (LO), Al Mueller/SS; 33 (UP), Kassia Halteman/SS; 33 (CTR), Linda Moore/NGYS; 33 (LO), Elliotte Rusty Harold/SS; **WESTERN BACKYARD:** 34-35, Guang Chow/NGYS; 36-37 (BACK), David Madison/GI; 36 (LE), Thy Bun/NGYS; 36 (RT), Gavin Emmons/NGYS; 37 (UP), Robert L Kothenbeutel/SS; 37 (CTR), Alejandro Herrera/NGYS; 37 (LO), May Woon/NGYS; 38, Brian Griffith/NGYS; 39 (UP), Paul Marto/NGYS; 39 (CTR), N. John Schmitt; 39 (LO), Thy Bun/NGYS; 40, Christopher Corman/NGYS; 41 (UP), Mark Zukowski/NGYS; 41 (CTR), Donald L. Malick; 41 (LO), Gavin Emmons/NGYS; 42, Quentin Furrow/NGYS; 43 (UP), May Woon/NGYS; 43 (CTR), N. John Schmitt; 43 (LO), May Woon/NGYS; 44, Lee F. Snyder/GI; 45 (UP), SaraJo/SS; 45 (CTR), H. Douglas Pratt; 45 (LO), Rolf Nussbaumer Photography/Alamy; 46, Robert L Kothenbeutel/SS; 47 (UP), Lesley Brown; 47 (CTR), Peter Burke; 47 (LO), Kristen Martyn; 48

(UP), Tom Reichner/SS; 48 (CTR), Mickey Samuni/NGYS; 48 (LO), Michael Ohaion/NGYS; 49 (UP), Kathrine Lloyd/NGYS; 49 (CTR), Ed Robertson/NGYS; 49 (LO), Tim Zurowski/SS; 50 (UP), raulbaenacasado/SS; 50 (CTR), Tim Zurowski/SS; 50 (LO), Steve & Dave Maslowski/GI; 51 (UP), teekaygee/SS; 51 (CTR), Shonn Morris/NGYS; 51 (LO), Tim Zurowski/SS; **CITY STREETS AND PARKS:** 52-53, Uri Rosenberg/NGYS; 54-55 (BACK), Walter Bibikow/GI; 54 (LE), Christine Haines/NGYS; 54 (RT), Joseph Rescinito/NGYS; 55 (UP RT), Akihiro Asami/NGYS; 55 (UP LE), Mary Ann Bridge/NGYS; 55 (LO), Jamie Link/NGYS; 56, Akihiro Asami/NGYS; 57 (UP), Patrick Lanham/NGYS; 57 (CTR), Donald L. Malick; 57 (LO), Luc Henri Fage/NGYS; 58, Steve Byland/SS; 59 (UP), Hide Inada/SS; 59 (CTR), Thomas R. Schultz; 59 (LO), RalphWilliam/Alamy Stock Photo; 60, Ron Storey/NGYS; 61 (UP), Gerome Dennie/NGYS; 61 (CTR), H. Douglas Pratt; 61 (LO), Mary Ann Bridge/NGYS; 62, Joseph Rescinito/NGYS; 63 (UP), Kathrine Lloyd/NGYS; 63 (CTR), H. Douglas Pratt; 63 (LO), Christina Quackenbush/NGYS; 64, Christine Haines/NGYS; 65 (UP), Elliott Neep/GI; 65 (CTR), N. John Schmitt; 65 (LO), Uri Rosenberg/NGYS; 66 (UP), Kristin Renbarger/NGYS; 66 (CTR), Steve and Dave Maslowski/GI; 66 (LO), Dennis Jacobsen/SS; 67 (UP), Mario Tizon/NGYS; 67 (CTR), Beverly Cochran/NGYS; 67 (LO), Toni Chowdhury/NGYS; **FARMS AND FIELDS:** 68-69, Mikael Johansson/NGYS; 70-71 (BACK), Shobeir Ansari/Flickr Open/GI; 70 (LE), James Cumming/NGYS; 70 (RT), Larry Keller/NGYS; 71 (UP), Vince Maidens/NGYS; 71 (CTR), Jim Zipp/GI; 71 (LO), Philip Haber/NGYS; 72, Tory Kallman/SS; 73 (UP), iwilliamSherman/Stockphoto/GI; 73 (CTR), Marc R. Hanson; 73 (LO), Patricio Robles Gil/Sierra Madre/Minden Pictures; 74, Vince Maidens/NGYS; 75 (UP), Alex Thomson/NGYS; 75 (CTR), Donald L. Malick; 75 (LO), Konrad Wothe/Minden Pictures; 76 (CTR), Jim Zipp/GI; 77 (UP), Boguslaw Brzyski/NGYS; 77 (CTR), N. John Schmitt; 77 (LO), Ron Storey/NGYS; 78, Cissy Beasley/NGYS; 79 (UP), Jan Galland/NGYS; 79 (CTR), H. Douglas Pratt; 79 (LO), Akihiro Asami/NGYS; 80, Raymond Barlow/NGYS; 81 (UP), janet furlong/NGYS; 81 (CTR), H. Douglas Pratt; 81 (LO), Larry Keller/NGYS; 82 (UP), Matthew Armanini/NGYS; 82 (CTR), Flickr Open/GI; 82 (LO), FotoRequest/SS; 83 (UP), Dave Karnes/NGYS; 83 (CTR), Bonnie Taylor Barry/SS; 83 (LO), Richard Cronberg/NGYS; **BEACH AND BAY:** 84-85, Jeff Maurtizen/NGP; 86-87 (BACK), Tim Fitzharris/Minden Pictures; 86 (LE), Bill Beckner/NGYS; 86 (RT), Jeff Mauritzen/NGP; 87 (UP), Vijayanand CD/NGYS; 87 (CTR), Linh Dinh/NGYS; 87 (LO), Andrea Lypka/NGYS; 88, Tim Zurowski/SS; 89 (UP), Frederick J. Horne/SS; 89 (CTR LE), Thomas R. Schultz; 89 (CTR RT), Daniel S. Smith; 89 (LO), Ivan Kuzmin/SS; 90, Daboost/SS; 91 (UP), Vijayanand CD/NGYS; 91 (CTR), Thomas R. Schultz; 91 (LO), Paul J Fusco/GI; 92, Tom Helinski/NGYS; 93 (UP), Boris Hristev/NGYS; 93 (CTR), Thomas R. Schultz; 93 (LO), Jim Gray/NGYS; 94, Jeff Mauritzen/NGP; 95 (UP), Dwight Sokoll/NGYS; 95 (CTR), Jonathan Alderfer; 95 (LO), Jeff Mauritzen/NGP; 96, Warren Sharpp/NGYS; 97 (UP), Steve Ellwood/NGYS; 97 (CTR), Donald L. Malick; 97 (LO), Michael Wulf/NGYS; 98 (UP), Kristine Lat/NGYS; 98 (CTR), Sunita Budhrani/NGYS; 98 (LO), Joseph Straccia/NGYS; 99 (UP), Ivan Kuzmin/SS; 99 (CTR), Aravind Krishnaswamy/NGYS; 99 (LO), Per Smitterberg/NGYS; **BIRDS IN PERIL:** 100-101, koji-hirano/SS; 102 (UP), Shane Rucker/NGYS; 102 (CTR), William Leaman/Alamy Stock Photo; 102 (LO), Mike DeBonis/NGYS; 103 (UP), Joshua Haviv/SS; 103 (CTR), Nature Photographers Ltd/Alamy Stock Photo; 103 (LO), Danita Delimont/Alamy Stock Photo; 104 (UP), FLPA/Alamy Stock Photo; 104 (CTR), Auscape International Pty Ltd/Alamy Stock Photo; 104 (LO), Martin Hale/FLPA/Minden Pictures; 105 (UP), Butterfly Hunter/SS; 105 (CTR), Tui De Roy/Minden Pictures; 105 (LO), Stephane Bidouze/SS; 106 (UP), Sleepy Lizard/SS; 106 (CTR), Steve Byland/SS; 106 (LO), Dave Azoulay/SS; 107 (UP), Tom Grundy/Alamy Stock Photo; 107 (CTR), Sari ONeal/SS; 107 (LO), Chris Howes/Wild Places Photography/Alamy Stock Photo; **SOUTHERN SWAMP AND BAYOU:** 108-109, Mike Delgado/NGYS; 110-111 (BACK), Gallo Images/Danita Delimont/GI; 110, Thomas LeClair/NGYS; 111 (UP LE), Michael Nichols/National Geographic Creative/GI; 111 (UP RT), Terry Piotraschke/NGYS; 111 (CTR), Steve Gettle/Minden Pictures; 111 (LO), Steve Ellwood/NGYS; 112, Steve Gettle/Minden Pictures; 113 (UP), Scott Leslie/Minden Pictures; 113 (CTR), Cynthia J. House; 113 (LO), Nathan Lovas Photography; 114, Terry Piotraschke/NGYS; 115 (UP), Francoise Macomber/NGYS; 115 (CTR), H. Jon Janosik; 115 (LO), Savannah Whitwam/NGYS; 116, Kris Docken/NGYS; 117 (UP), Phil Reid/SS; 117 (CTR), Diane Pierce; 117 (LO), Thomas LeClair/NGYS; 118, Bildagentur Zoonar GmbH/SS; 119 (UP), Jeff Holcombe/SS; 119 (CTR), Marc R. Hanson; 119 (LO), Laurel A Egan/SS; 120, Derek Dafoe/NGYS; 121 (UP), Michael Nichols/National Geographic Creative/GI; 121 (CTR), Donald L. Malick; 121 (LO), Michael Nichols/National Geographic Creative/GI; 122 (UP), Glenn Price/SS; 122 (CTR), Vladimir Kalinovsky/NGYS; 122 (LO), Teresa Darragh/NGYS; 123 (UP), Visuals Unlimited, Inc./John Cornell/GI; 123 (CTR), Hideta Nagai/NGYS; 123 (LO), Mark Lewer/NGYS; **RIVER AND MARSH:** 124-125, Sandor Bernath/NGYS; 126-127 (BACK), Raymond Gehman/National Geographic Creative/GI; 126 (LE), Double Brow Imagery/SS; 126 (RT), Gregory Johnston/SS; 127 (UP LE), Raymond Barlow/NGYS; 127 (UP RT), Nick Chill/NGYS; 127 (LO), Edward Mattis/NGYS; 128, Randy Rimland/SS; 129 (UP), Harlan Humphrey/NGYS; 129 (CTR), Donald L. Malick;129 (LO), John Sutton/NGYS; 130, Bruce Leonard/iStockphoto; 131 (UP), John Starsja/NGYS; 131 (CTR), Donald L. Malick; 131 (LO), Yoshikatsu Nagaya/NGYS; 132, Steve Ellwood/NGYS; 133 (UP), Ike Austin/NGYS; 133 (CTR), Donald L. Malick; 133 (LO), Monika Petersen/NGYS; 134, Double Brow Imagery/SS; 135 (UP), Rick & Nora Bowers/Alamy Stock Photo; 135 (CTR), Thomas R. Schultz; 135 (LO), Susan Gary Photography/Moment RF/GI; 136, Glenn Young/SS; 137 (UP), Steve Creek/NGYS; 137 (CTR), H. Douglas Pratt; 137 (LO), Edward Mattis/NGYS; 138 (UP), Dennis Gazso/NGYS; 138 (CTR), Tony Britton/SS; 138 (LO), Martin Knippel/NGYS; 139 (UP), Sandor Bernath/NGYS; 139 (CTR), Cosmin Nahaiciuc/NGYS; 139 (LO), NFKenyon/SS; **PRAIRIE AND PLAINS:** 140-141, Steven Smith/NGYS; 142-143 (BACK), Kellie L. Folkerts/SS; 142 (LE), Brian E Kushner/SS; 142 (RT), Donald M. Jones/Minden Pictures; 143 (UP), Steve & Dave Maslowski/GI; 143 (CTR), Mike Kuran/SS; 143 (LO), Wim Weenink/Minden Pictures; 144, Keneva Photography/SS; 145 (UP), Rusty Dodson/SS; 145 (CTR LE), Killian Mullarney; 145 (CTR RT), Daniel S. Smith; 145 (LO), Kimberley McClard/SS; 146, Graham Owen/NGYS; 147 (UP), Stubblefield Photography/SS; 147 (CTR), Donald L. Malick; 147 (LO), Matthew Armanini/NGYS; 148, All Canada Photos/Alamy; 149 (UP), John Stankewitz/NGYS; 149 (CTR), Jonathan Alderfer; 149 (LO), Jim Zipp/GI; 150, Stephen Dalton/Minden Pictures; 151 (UP), Dietmar Nill/NGYS; 151 (CTR), H. Douglas Pratt; 151 (LO), Wim Weenink/Minden Pictures; 152, Photo Researchers/GI; 153 (UP), Wayne Lynch/GI; 153 (CTR), Thomas R. Schultz; 153 (LO), Rolf Nussbaumer/NPL/Minden Pictures; 154 (UP), All Canada Photos RM/GI; 154 (CTR), Noelle Zaleski/NGYS; 154 (LO), Donald M. Jones/Minden Pictures; 155 (UP), John Stankewitz/NGYS; 155 (CTR), Marcel van Kammen/Foto Natura/Minden Pictures; 155 (LO), Markus Varesvuo/NPL/Minden Pictures; **DESERTS:** 156-157, William Leaman/Alamy; 158-159 (BACK), Paul B. Moore/SS; 158 (LE), Takahashi Photography/SS; 158 (RT), Owen Newman/GI; 159 (UP), Nasim Mansurov/NGYS; 159 (CTR), Alexander Viduetsky/NGYS; 159 (LO), Danita Delimont/GI; 160, David Tipling/NPL/Minden Pictures; 161 (UP), Konrad Wothe/Minden Pictures; 161 (CTR), H. Douglas Pratt; 161 (LO), Danita Delimont/GI; 162, Takahashi Photography/SS; 163 (UP), Mark Newman/Lonely Planet Images/GI; 163 (CTR BOTH), N. John Schmidt; 163 (LO), Alan Murphy/BIA/Minden Pictures; 164, Tom Vezo/Minden Pictures; 165 (UP), Cyril Ruoso/JH Editorial/Minden Pictures; 165 (CTR), N. John Schmitt; 165 (LO), Rolf Nussbaumer/NPL/Minden Pictures; 166, Tom Vezo/Minden Pictures; 167 (UP), Jim Zipp/GI; 167 (CTR), Donald L. Malick; 167 (LO), Owen Newman/GI; 168, Jared Hobbs; 169 (UP), Walter Meayers Edwards/National Geographic Creative/GI; 169 (CTR), H. Douglas Pratt; 169 (LO), Nature/UIG/GI; 170 (UP), SuperStock/Alamy; 170 (CTR), Anton Foltin/SS; 170 (LO), All Canada Photos/Alamy; 171 (UP), Angel Di Bilio/NGYS; 171 (CTR), Cissy Beasley/NGYS; 171 (LO), Stubblefield Photography/SS; **WESTERN MOUNTAINS:** 172-173, Konrad Wothe/Minden Pictures; 174-175 (BACK), Rudy Balasko/SS; 174 (LE), Ernest Ross/NGYS; 174 (RT), Tom Vezo/Minden Pictures; 175 (UP), Werner Bollmann/GI; 175 (CTR), Dena Miller/NGYS; 175 (LO), Jeff Brubaker/NGYS; 176, Raymond Barlow/NGYS; 177 (UP), Guy Edwardes/GI; 177 (CTR), Donald L. Malick; 177 (LO), David Madison/GI; 178, Tom Vezo/Minden Pictures; 179 (UP), Roy H. Photography/Flickr RF/GI; 179 (CTR), H. Douglas Pratt; 179 (LO), Larsen Calvin/GI; 180, David Parsons/iStock-photo/GI; 181 (UP), Mary Plage/Oxford Scientific RM/GI; 181 (CTR), H. Douglas Pratt; 181 (LO), Matthew Driver/Alamy Stock Photo; 182, Dena Miller/NGYS;183 (UP), Walter Nussbaumer/NGYS; 183 (CTR), H. Douglas Pratt; 183 (LO), Tom Vezo/Minden Pictures; 184, Bob Smith/National Geographic Creative/GI; 185 (UP), Charles Melton/Alamy; 185 (CTR), Peter Burke; 185 (LO), Bob Cochran/NGYS; 186 (UP), Catherine Ashbee/NGYS; 186 (CTR), Jack Milchanowski/Visuals Unlimited, Inc./GI; 186 (LO), Glen Bartley/GI; 187 (UP), Scot Heath/NGYS; 187 (CTR), M-C-C/iStockphoto/GI; 187 (LO), Enrique Rabelo/NGYS; **ROCK STAR BIRDS:** 188-189, Vince Maidens/NGYS; 190 (UP), Robert Biondo/NGYS; 190 (CTR), critterbiz/SS; 190 (LO), Bill Dodsworth/NGYS; 191 (UP), jpetersen/SS; 191 (CTR), Pierre Larouche/NGYS; 191 (LO), Steve Byland/SS; 192 (UP), Gary Vestal/GI; 192 (CTR), Keith Szafranski/iStockphoto; 192 (LO), James Hale; 193 (UP), Jeff Mauritzen/NGP; 193 (CTR), robert mcgillivray/SS; 193 (LO), worldswild-lifewonders/SS; 194 (UP), Jo Crebbin/SS; 194 (CTR), Wolfgang Kruck/SS; 194 (LO), AndreAnita/SS; 195 (UP), Rick & Nora Bowers/Alamy Stock Photo; 195 (CTR), Steve Byland/SS; 195 (LO), Piotr Krzeslak/iStockphoto/GI; **END MATTER:** 196-201 (ALL), Lori Epstein/NG Staff; 202 (ALL), Jonathan Alderfer

Credits

For Zora and Carly with love.

Published by National Geographic Partners, LLC.

Since 1888, the National Geographic Society has funded
more than 14,000 research, conservation, education,
and storytelling projects around the world. National
Geographic Partners distributes a portion of the funds
it receives from your purchase to National Geographic
Society to support programs including the conservation
of animals and their habitats. To learn more, visit
natgeo.com/info.

For more information, visit nationalgeographic.com,
call 1-877-873-6846, or write to the following address:

National Geographic Partners, LLC
1145 17th Street N.W.
Washington, DC 20036-4688 U.S.A.

For librarians and teachers: nationalgeographic.com/
books/librarians-and-educators

More for kids from National Geographic:
natgeokids.com

For rights or permissions inquiries, please contact
National Geographic Books Subsidiary Rights:
bookrights@natgeo.com

Designed by Brett Challos

National Geographic supports K–12 educators with
ELA Common Core Resources. Visit natgeoed.org/
commoncore for more information.

Library of Congress Cataloging-in-Publication Data

Names: Alderfer, Jonathan K., author. | National
    Geographic Society (U.S.)
Title: National Geographic Kids bird guide of North
    America / by Jonathan Alderfer.
Other titles: Bird guide of North America
Description: Second edition. | Washington, DC :
    National Geographic Kids, [2018] | Audience: Ages
    8-12. | Audience: Grades 4 to 6.
Identifiers: LCCN 2017035093| ISBN 9781426330735
    (pbk.) | ISBN 9781426330742 (hardcover)
Subjects: LCSH: Birds--North America--Identification--
    Juvenile literature.
Classification: LCC QL715 .A433 2018 | DDC 598.097--dc23
LC record available at https://lccn.loc.gov/2017035093

Printed in the United States of America
21/QCG/4 (paperback)
21/QCG/2 (RLB)

ACKNOWLEDGMENTS

I'd like to thank all of the editorial and design staff at National Geographic Kids Books for their expertise
and guidance. Priyanka Lamichhane, my patient editor, was a pleasure to work with and skillfully kept the
project on point and on schedule. My wife, Zora Margolis, gently guided me with editorial advice and made
numerous suggestions that greatly improved the text. She leavened my writing with her wit and sense of
language in ways that I would never have thought of on my own. Thank you.

—Jonathan Alderfer